# IT IS NOW FOR YOU TO
# CHANGE!
## FOR DEVELOPMENT OF
# INDIAN
## INDUSTRY

**SHUNSUKE TSUDA, NARESH CHACHRA
SANJAY BAGARIA**

INDIA • SINGAPORE • MALAYSIA

## Notion Press

Old No. 38, New No. 6
McNichols Road, Chetpet
Chennai - 600 031

First Published by Notion Press 2020
Copyright © Shunsuke Tsuda, Naresh Chachra & Sanjay Bagaria 2020
All Rights Reserved.

ISBN 978-1-64249-278-1

This book has been published with all efforts taken to make the material error-free after the consent of the author. However, the author and the publisher do not assume and hereby disclaim any liability to any party for any loss, damage, or disruption caused by errors or omissions, whether such errors or omissions result from negligence, accident, or any other cause.

While every effort has been made to avoid any mistake or omission, this publication is being sold on the condition and understanding that neither the author nor the publishers or printers would be liable in any manner to any person by reason of any mistake or omission in this publication or for any action taken or omitted to be taken or advice rendered or accepted on the basis of this work. For any defect in printing or binding the publishers will be liable only to replace the defective copy by another copy of this work then available.

# CONTENTS

*Preface* ............................................................................................ 7
*Acknowledgments* ....................................................................... 11

1. **Potential of India** ................................................................. 13

    1.1 Liberalization of the Economy ...................................... 13
    1.2 The Automotive Industry ............................................... 14

2. **Export Comes First** .............................................................. 18

    2.1 The Development of Tertiary Industry ......................... 18
    2.2 IT is Limited ..................................................................... 19
    2.3 The Ability to Bring Improvement in
         Manufacturing Is a Key ................................................... 20
    2.4 Export Comes First .......................................................... 21

3. **How Did Toyota Become the No. 1 in the World?** ......... 23

## 4. Problems of India ................................................................ 28

4.1 What Do You Mean By 'Indian Quality'? .......................28
4.2 Rupee ...............................................................................30
4.3 The Quality of Indian Products and Services ...............31

## 5. Good Points of India ........................................................... 35

5.1 Rich Population is Good ................................................35
5.2 The Indian Is Expected ..................................................36

## 6. Why Do Quality Problems Occur in India? ...................... 38

6.1 Mild Climate and Abundant Food ...............................38
6.2 The Gods Might Be Angry ............................................39
6.3 No Pain, No Gain ..........................................................40

## 7. What Make Things Difficult to Succeed? .......................... 42

7.1 The Problems in the Indian Manufacturing Sector ...42
7.2 Historic Issues ................................................................44
7.3 Protected Industry .........................................................45
7.4 Way of Thinking ............................................................45
7.5 Consumer Attitude ........................................................47
7.6 How to Improve the Situation? .....................................48
7.7 Why Don't We Return to the Basics in the Long Run? ...49
7.8 It Is Good to Learn ........................................................50
7.9 We Need More Practice .................................................52

## 8. What Should Be Learned from Toyota? ............................ 54

8.1 The First Is Human Resources .....................................54
8.2 The Importance of Basics ..............................................56
8.3 The Original of All ........................................................57
8.4 You Can Learn from Daily Life ....................................66
8.5 Lean and Waste ..............................................................80

| 8.6 | Seven Wastes of TPS | 82 |
| 8.7 | Mainstream | 93 |
| 8.8 | Visual Control | 100 |
| 8.9 | Flexible Manpower | 106 |
| 8.10 | Other Important Points | 112 |

## 9. How Do We Succeed in India? ............................................. 117

| 9.1 | How Much Ability Does a Human Being Have? | 117 |
| 9.2 | Why Can't Human Beings Communicate Well? | 118 |
| 9.3 | Equality Among Humans and in Profession | 120 |
| 9.4 | Bottom-Up Industries | 121 |
| 9.5 | Power of Dreams | 122 |
| 9.6 | Power of Love | 124 |
| 9.7 | Power of Direction | 125 |

## 10. An Organization That May Be Successful in the Global Market ............................................. 128

| 10.1 | Safety First | 128 |
| 10.2 | Thoroughness of 5S | 129 |
| 10.3 | The Organization to Speak on Dreams | 131 |
| 10.4 | The Organization That Makes the Most of Education | 132 |
| 10.5 | Accurate Information Management | 134 |
| 10.6 | A Group of Professionals | 135 |
| 10.7 | Be Mindful of Gratitude | 136 |
| 10.8 | Be Proud of You | 137 |

## 11. Closing ............................................. 139

*"Progress is impossible without change, and those who cannot change their mind, cannot change anything"*

**George Bernard Shaw**

*"Alone We Can Do So Little; Together We Can Do So Much"*

**Helen Keller**

# PREFACE

We, including a Japanese consultant with more than ten years of experience in India, are sure that India with its abundance of human talent, resources and diversity will lead the world in future, in a different way from China. Even though the advancement is moderate due to still unresolved issues of labor reforms, land acquisitions, erratic power availability and taxation anomalies, many sectors have shown promise of growth. The government's new thrust on 'Make in India' and ease of doing business is a step in the right direction but it is taking time to bring positive results, may be due to the intricacies of being the largest democratic country in the world. However, a positive movement is steady and sure.

Young Indians, who had worked in the Silicon Valley, fuelled a revolution in intellectual technology in the country more than two decades ago. They contributed much to the export and growth of India after having satisfied American and European customers using English as the common language and proving their command in the field of information technology. We should also recognize that India's IT industries now face big competition from emerging countries with regard to productivity and cost.

There is no doubt that the expectation is similar for a revolution in agriculture and manufacturing.

Somehow, the contribution of these sectors in GDP growth is not sufficient for the size of the nation. Being a part of and having contributed to Japan manufacturing excellence, we firmly believe that India has huge potential to grow if it analyzes all key issues and learns from the experiences of other countries, including Japan. We feel that this is the key for the economic growth of India.

There are a lot of textbooks on Japanese management system available in Indian bookstores and on the internet. Some Japanese consultants are actually working in Indian industries. Even though the management of companies in India appreciates such practices, there seem to be a lot of cases where Japanese management system is not working in actual manufacturing sites. In this book, we are pursuing what we should do to identify gaps and overcome challenges, looking at the kind of problems that are hindrances for the Indian manufacturing industries to grow.

In this book, the essence of TPS (Toyota Production System,) which you should first understand, is explained completely instead of just explaining the theoretical methods available elsewhere. We hope all readers understand the essence along with the methods. This book is written based on the impression of Japanese managers as well as the ideas of their Indian counterparts who had worked in Japanese companies.

It is of vital importance to study the successes of Toyota and others in order for India to lead the world. The company is staying ahead of the game due to its productivity. It has created its own methods to enhance productivity. The methods have become subjects to be learnt around the world. What is interesting is that it is not concealing the methods, because the company knows these methods are not mastered easily and need to be adapted into the culture of the company. You can't get the real fruit with just the imitation of the methods. Many companies in the world face this difficulty. An Indian company is also not an exception.

The common point that contemporary and world-leading companies seem to understand is that employees are human beings as well as customers. The most important aspect is finding ways to utilize human powers, factoring their potential abilities. We would like to try and explain this diligently. We hope readers understand this essence thoroughly and contribute to their own development, thereby to the economic growth of India.

*"Before cars, make people"*

Eiji Toyoda
President Toyota Motor Corporation

TPS is the production system developed by Toyota Motor Corporation to provide best quality, lowest cost and shortest lead time through the elimination of waste

*Dear Readers,*

*Thanks for your interests in this book. Authors have always felt intense need for change in order to remain competitive and relevant. This book is a small effort in that direction, through which we have shared our thoughts and experiences to encourage readers to develop their own road map for desired change. Many simple and practical examples have been elucidated, coming out of our work exposure with Japanese/Indian Industries. We hope readers will benefit and successfully meet challenges of global business cultures and environment. We also hope that readers will take advantage of the book, whenever they encounter similar situation in their daily work and personal lives.*

*Also, we welcome comments of readers and suggestions. Please feel free to communicate your daily situations and progress at changenowfordevelopment@gmail.com*

*Never stop learning and challenging yourself and never give up on your dreams.*

# Acknowledgments

The Japanese consultant has wanted to write this booklet since long. He was reluctant as he does not write English well and Indian readers might not understand what he wants to communicate. His English language skill is comparable to that of a junior high school student in Japan. However, he tried hard to write in English, consulting a dictionary while at it. He was also afraid that he may not have entirely understood the culture of India. Later on, two Indian consultants with considerable experience in Japanese companies joined him. Many Japanese and Indian friends have also supported him.

    Hideo Ide, S.K. Manna, Archana Shankar Mathur, Ratan Vaid, Ravinder Kumar, Digital Hive, Naresh Kantoor & Ashok K Mittal also contributed to shape the book.

    Poems by Shunsuke Tsuda and Vaidya Ratnakar

    Chorus from JIT Laboratory and Translated by Shunsuke Tsuda

## References

1. Toyota Production System, Taichi Ohno
2. Toyota Production System, Shigenori Kotani
3. The Life-Changing Magic of Tidying up, Marie Kondo
4. My Life and Work, Henry Ford
5. Today and Tomorrow, Henry Ford
6. Cleaning Angels in Bullet Trains, Isao Endo
7. HouRenSou Makes the Company Strong, Tomiji Yamazaki

Co-authors
Shunsuke Tsuda
Naresh Chachra
Sanjay Bagaria

# –1–

# POTENTIAL OF INDIA

As we mentioned before, India will surely become a world economic leader or at least one with an influence on the world economy. We need to understand the history and circumstances of the Indian economy.

## 1.1 Liberalization of the Economy

Until 1991, India was going through economic chaos. Poor productivity of public sector enterprises and a socialism-driven non-competitive market policy had prevented the improvement of quality and technology in Indian industries. Japan bulged up the bubble economy that burst in the same year. Also, around the same time the Gulf War started. Oil prices soared. The remittance from non-resident Indians working in Middle East decreased and India's foreign exchange reserves were running out. The Indian government understood the crisis and tried to procure an emergency loan from the International Monetary Fund with the help of USA, Japan and Germany. But the loan was frozen due to the political turmoil in India.

In light of this national and international scenario, the then Congress government in 1991 introduced new economic and industrial reforms.

The New Industrial Policy was introduced. The government's budgetary constraints could not provide funds for investment. The government steered towards the introduction of foreign capital. This driving force boosted India's GDP. But the vulnerability of the economy to external factors such as the Lehman shock showed, and there were many voices seeking further liberalization of the economy.

In 2013, the Indian GDP growth rate went down to 6.39% percent. In 2014, a new government emerged with new hope of accelerated growth of the Indian economy. Now the growth rate of GDP has already overtaken China's and is number 1 in the world. As per the World Bank, India has now overtaken France to become the sixth-largest economy in the world. Its per capita grew from USD 1,430 in 2010 to USD 1,805 in 2015 and reached USD 2,046 in March 2019. The potential is likely to increase in future.

## 1.2 The Automotive Industry

Historically, India has not had a good record of development in the domestic automotive industry. Before the entry of Suzuki, only two brands of cars—Ambassador and Fiat—were being assembled in India. The Maruti Suzuki's case has been a big success in a joint venture between India and abroad in a sense. The joint venture between the Indian Government and Japan's Suzuki Motor happened nine years prior to economic liberalization in 1991. GM and Ford started assembly of completely knocked down vehicles in India much earlier in 1928 and 1930 respectively. GM and Ford had to withdraw from India once in between because of various regulations but they landed back in India after the restrictions on foreign investments were eased off.

Maruti Suzuki could realize the dream of the 'Indian small car concept' with a dream project in collaboration with the Suzuki car company in Japan. A small and beautiful car called Maruti 800 was produced as a result of the joint effort between Indian technicians under the guidance of the Japanese management, which became a big hit in India and transformed the automotive scenario of the country. Maruti Suzuki was a suitable model for the middle-class people who were becoming richer due to the growth in IT and other industries. Due to the low cost and compact size, they preferred to buy the Maruti car instead of motorcycles or other two-wheelers. Four-wheeler vehicle sales in India until around 2000 had been less than 1 million units per year, but since 2003, it has shown a rapid growth. The increase in the population of the middle class due to the proliferation of the IT industry and attaining better purchasing power might have had a big impact on the economic spur. Over 1 million four-wheeler units were sold in 2004 and close to 2 million units in 2007. The economic growth of China and India shocked the world.

However, a big worldwide recession in 2008 affected India as well. In 2008, India registered a slower growth in commercial vehicle sales at one point. Although India's passenger vehicle sales recorded a growth of 25.6 percent in 2009 and 29.4 percent in 2010, it decelerated in 2011 and 2014. We should know that India's economy is intensely volatile. It does not seem to have an underlying strength. Now more than thirteen foreign and local automobile manufacturers are competing fiercely with each other. The severe competition in the automotive industry could help develop technologies. Further economic development can be achieved by producing vehicles that could cater to the domestic market as well as be exported, which is currently underway. In 2016 about 3.4 million four-wheeler vehicles were sold and 654 thousands were exported.

Between April 2000 and December 2016, the Indian automobile industry attracted foreign direct investment (FDI) of around USD 16 billion. And even as we write this book, reports say that Honda Cars India Ltd is planning to invest around USD 59.24 million to increase its production capacity by 50 percent (to 180,000 units.)

The government is focusing on developing a policy framework to support electric vehicle start-ups. The newly introduced GST will support lower raw material cost. We could say that we are on track to development.

Further, the Indian auto industry became the 4th largest in the world with sales of 4.02 million units (excluding two-wheelers) in 2017. At the same time, India was the 7th largest manufacturer of commercial vehicles in 2017.

With a growing middle class and a growing interest in rural markets, the two-wheeler segment is expanding. India also has strong export growth expectations. Automobile exports grew 15.54 per cent during April 2018-February 2019. In addition, the major automobile players in the Indian market are expected to make India a leader in the two-wheeler and four – wheeler markets in the world by 2020.

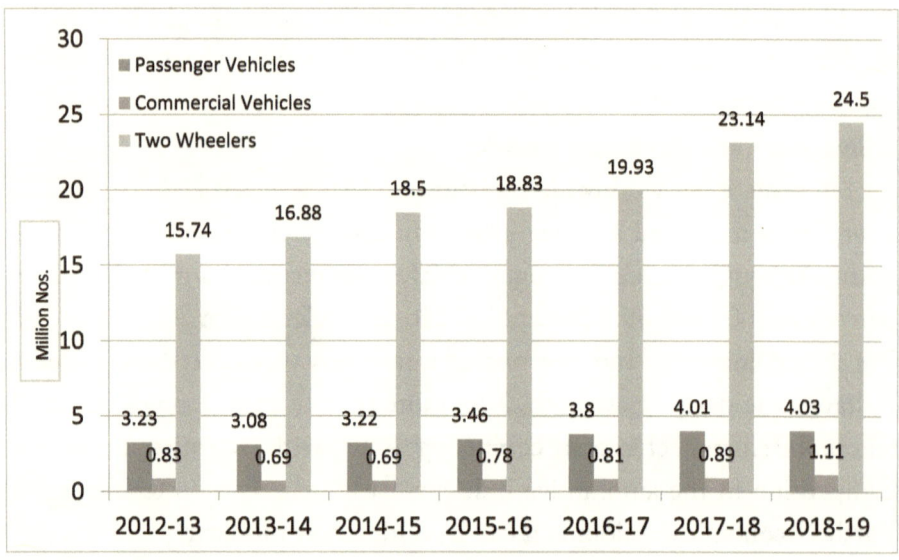

**Growth of Automobile Sector in India (in Million Numbers)**

However recent trends of volatility of automobile sales in India, is disturbing. Weakening demand and resulting challenges has complicated growth path of auto sector. Sudden change in consumer behaviour and massive technology changes in the pipeline has put a brake. India faced worst sales slowdown in recent history, resulting into inventory pile up and affecting profitability of the companies. Auto and its ancillaries are still labour intensive in India. Report of job losses and uncertainty forced all major companies to chalk out their future strategies.

The Indian automobile business contributes 49% of manufacturing GDP while supporting almost 37 million jobs. Its continuous growth in consumption and exports is extremely critical to enhance our GDP and achieve ambitious targets.

While government will bring out a set of new policies on taxes and boosters for auto industry, there is lot to be done within the plants. We need more than before proper and disciplined utilisation of our resources, especially young talented manpower we have. Eliminating all wastages is the key in converting "crisis into opportunity" and remain competitive.

### How Toyota Handled Recession in 2008:

Toyota is known to treat its people as assets. Its response to recession in 2008 was not to lay off any permanent employees, as was the case with many other Automobile companies; neither did it impact supplier relations.

Toyota instead reduced work hours and negotiated temporary pay cuts. At the same time utilized opportunity to introduce new measures to improve profitability and flexibility. Like reduce breakeven point of its plants from 80% to 70% of capacity. It was something of a huge challenge for the company that was already pioneering lean.

# –2–

# EXPORT COMES FIRST

## 2.1 The Development of Tertiary Industry

The IT industry was, in fact, what revolutionized the Indian economy. The GDP of India was not being pushed up by primary industries like agriculture and fisheries. Even secondary industries like manufacturing, had minimal effect. Growth was largely due to tertiary industries like service. The Indian IT industry has been offering software development services to overseas customers. It seems this kind of development in the service sector was not completely new. In fact, India had started providing services to the outside world much earlier, around 1974. However, it could not be a pioneer in the domestic market, in the tertiary industry segment of communication. As a result of this, the mobile connection numbers have only now reached a level of more than one billion.

We need to pause and think with a cool mind at this point. What is the natural course of development of the industry? First, the primary industry, which is vital to life maintenance, should be developed. The next important thing is to develop the secondary industries, which increase the convenience of our lives and work. And finally the tertiary industries that can provide us richer and more comfortable lives. Of course, we may think it could happen simultaneously or a reverse progression of the above sequence may be more acceptable, but the key principle is as follows. It might seem like an extreme expression. Human beings can survive without the secondary and tertiary industries if the primary industry is developed sufficiently. But the vice versa can't be true. In other words, the primary industry is the foundation of the country. As human beings, we have to advance the technology aiding food supply, and we have to supply food to every person. When we have extra food, we can provide for the other countries in need.

The tertiary industry contribute more than 50 percent of India's GDP and is currently the backbone of the Indian economy. It means that India is a service-oriented country, which can also provide professional services. However, we have to be careful about determining if Indian tertiary industries are actually providing world-class services in all areas? Do the services really satisfy all foreign and Indian customers? Isn't it true that a lot of foreigners are not satisfied with the services provided by India? We feel that the tourism industry, the most typical tertiary industry, should grow more progressively. India, with a rich cultural heritage, has the potential of growing the tourism business to the level of the IT business. We sincerely hope that people here ponder on what is wrong and what has been missing in the past.

## 2.2 IT is Limited

The IT industry has been growing at a great pace, but the growth rate seems to have decelerated lately. India's IT companies are struggling with emerging competitors like Philippines, Canada and Poland. By reflecting on whether or not we have problems about quality and services in software development, we have a chance of getting a strong business status.

IT contributed to the exports in India. The GDP of tertiary industries play a big part. But we should understand that only a few people are working in this field. The IT industry is absorbing only 200,000 to 300,000 young candidates annually even though more than 15 million pass out every year. The important thing to recognize is that the prosperity in the field was achieved thanks to language, the experience of excellent Indians in Silicon Valley, the utilization of time differences, and the lower cost of domestic engineers.

Now we should deliberate on whether the foreign customers were attracted by the quality of the product or the cheap cost. In order to prosper more, the IT industry is also expected to improve in management. Now it is time we considered IT as a manufacturing industry instead of a service.

**An Indian IT Company**

## 2.3 The Ability to Bring Improvement in Manufacturing Is a Key

The majority of citizens of any country are engaged in the primary and secondary industries. These industries are termed 'monozukuri' in Japanese, which loosely translates to 'how to make things'. This refers to a professional's job of making things. The professional job is the process of achieving maximum output through minimum input. Input refers to the total energy required to produce the product (the commodity in manufacturing) that satisfies a customer, and the output is the degree of satisfaction that a customer derives. In the case of manufacturing, any number of professionals could be involved in improving the monozukuri. As competency of manufacturing improves the economy develops, thus spearheading a monozukuri revolution.

**Monozukuri is like a Craftsman's Work**

## 2.4 Export Comes First

India has surpassed Thailand in rice export to become the number 1 exporter in the world. India is also a top producer of banana and milk and is a self-sufficient country in food production. A primary industry is directly linked to the people's life. It gets the overall priority. Recently, the tertiary industry, which India's economy is relying so much on, has been on a decline. India's trade is still suffering from deficits. Secondary industries such as automobile manufacturing are yet to attain their full potential and reach global standards. Foreign investors are still evaluating possibilities of investments in new projects. The rupee has been under pressure. More than fifteen million young people pass out every year. It is an abundant labor force in a way. But without creation of enough job opportunities, mass unemployment may be generated. A small number of taxpayers alone cannot afford to take care of unemployed people. The recent introduction of GST and other tax reforms are likely to ensure more people come into the tax net, so that the majority pay more taxes.

We know the relation between currency and exports and that an increase in export means better currency value. At the same time, weaker currency should also boost exports. The way to come out of such a cycle is by boosting the quality and function of India's products. Unless this happens, the rupee value can't increase in true meaning. In the case of Japan, during the period when a fixed exchange rate was imposed, the export expanded drastically due to the low cost. Large quantities of Japanese products went into the American markets until America finally screamed. The currency exchange system was allowed to float in 1973. The yen, which was valued at 360 against a dollar, started going up. Whenever the value of yen went up, Japan's exporters faced difficulty. But instead of complaining, they took great efforts to improve their productivity. Now, even with the rate of 100 yen per dollar, Japan's exporters have the ability to compete in the global market. **We think the pursuit for quality, services and productivity is inevitably required for India's economic development.**

There is an imbalance in the current situation of India. We think India can take the right steps to correct it. Currently, India's economy is very vulnerable. The strength of India's economy is subject to increase in overseas funding by foreign investors and reaping the benefits. India's economy needs strengthening so that it can withstand tremors and shakes, to grow further. We need to do the groundwork firmly. And we should step up to the situation where we are able to export products to the global market.

A weak rupee against the dollar makes import costlier. India still imports its major oil requirement. We need to develop competitive exports to have a correct balance for a sustained economy.

India at the same time also has the potential for manufacturing and being a distribution hub for markets in Africa, Middle East and Europe.

> *"Get Closer than ever to your customers. So close that you tell them what they need well before they realize it themselves"*
>
> Steve Jobs

### Importance of Exports in an Economy:

Growth of an economy is directly related to exports. If exports increase faster as compared to imports, the economy will surely become developed economy. At the same time instable exports effect the economic development.

Lower exports mean low foreign exchange earnings which in turn means lessor purchasing capacity of the country. Efficiency of investments rise with exports creating growth and economic stability.

# –3–

# HOW DID TOYOTA BECOME THE NO. 1 IN THE WORLD?

To understand "How did Toyota become No. 1 in the world" lets study the backdrop briefly.

Toyota was founded by Sakichi Toyota, who had started company by making automatic weaving machine. He wanted to fuel industrialization in Japan. So he entrusted his son, Kiichiro Toyota to produce cars towards industrialization. Kiichiro Toyota firstly set up a lab in 1930, and began to work on development of the car.

Soon after the war, Kiichiro Toyota wanted to catch up with the United States in car production. Toyota vice president, Taichi Ono, believed they needed ten times or more improvement of productivity, in order to catch up with the United States automobile production. Thus Toyota started to invent and develop the Toyota Production System.

At that stage it was possible to assemble cars only during the last ten days of each month. This is because first 20 days of the month were spent in collection of all parts required for production. Or in other words it was the month-end production technique.

Kiichiro Toyota thought the best way forward was that each part was gathered in the "just-in-time" for the assembly operation of the car. Taichi Ono, who was assigned this task, worked hard on this as this way the production of vehicles would become possible from the beginning of the month. The concept of the "just-in-time" was further improved repeatedly.

A production method Kanban, which improved all past production systems was invented, and started in 1962. This Kanban system was followed and improved for about 20 years to become the base of the Toyota Production System.

After the first oil crisis of 1973 there was massive recession. And the world came to recognize Toyota Production System. The reason why TPS became get attention was that Toyota recovered to profit very quickly.

Let's also study GM and Ford of the United States who have led the world in the automotive Industry in their own way. They rolled out lower-priced cars and contributed to economic growth. Mass production and the flow assembly line operation showed results. We need to study their efforts from a historical viewpoint, just like the Industrial Revolution. Is it a coincidence that Toyota and a few others, which are leading the world now, are brands from countries that suffered losses in World War II? Toyota at least must have met the target with a hungry spirit saying, "Catch up with America and overtake!" We can't deny the power that they have contributed to the revival of their home countries ruined by the defeat in war. We should not forget that a man can show exemplary power in a given trying circumstance. There is a concept of "Craftsmanship" in Japan and 'Meister' in Germany. It is a concept of being a master of a technical skill. This is the concept of monozukuri. There is a saying, "The enterprise is the person," in Japan. There are various ways to translate this. According to our understanding the most important work of the top management is to create as many professionals as possible.

Henry Ford, who is the founder of Ford Motor Company, says, "Materials are less important than human beings." It is man who makes the defect. It is man who sends erroneous information. It is man who stops the line. Toyota has brought up their people and created a lot of professionals in the enterprise. This is the truth in other sectors like IT too, not just the automotive.

**Craftsmanship or Professional Work**

Presently Toyota is the top automotive company in the world and it will remain there for decades to come. Why not? The entire organization practices same principles and encourage similar work culture. In Toyota no one is bigger or superior to organization. Most of the leaders work extremely hard in sustaining and improving daily work habits of their teams, in the true spirits of learnings from founders.

Toyota, which started as a family company, has continued with a legacy to pursue perfection in all spheres of their activities. The company has succeeded in instilling in all employees a burning desire to be the best. They succeeded in creating groups of people who are humble, practical and ahead of times, changed the work environment. Respecting and honouring their employees the company changed the meaning of successful organization.

The organization put massive efforts in developing their people, focusing all energy for betterment of society and their country. With this kind of unique approach, Toyota became no 1 company which stands today as most admired and growing organization.

Since beginning, like any other major company Toyota also had its share of quality issues, recalls, recession and other global upheavals. However so strong were their beliefs in the principles of their founders, that with time they only became subject of study and research.

We are aware of numerous Japanese business practices, always aiming to change for improvement. With several decades of success, concept of Monozukari has become their way of life. When translated from Japanese, Monozukuri literally means 'production' or 'making of things'. In a broader sense, however, it embodies a synthesis of know how and spirit of Japan's manufacturing practices. Monozukari ultimately emphasises on working and creating innovation together.

Monozukuri encourages workers to 'bring their mind to work'. They are fully empowered and trained to deal with different situations to create an elevated sense of ownership. It is about making products as well as about instilling pride and passion about their jobs. It requires creative minds and is often related to craftsmanship that can be earned through lengthy apprenticeship practice rather than the structured curricula taught at traditional schools. Monozukuri represents the maker's philosophy of how to make the product - the philosophy that is deeply rooted in Japanese tradition in manufacturing. It can be said that Monozukuri is a philosophy rather than technique or method. Characteristically, every facet of Japan's life - from architecture, design, food, and fashion to social rituals - has an underlying philosophy, and the Japanese people can translate those philosophical ideas into production.

Before cars, make people" is a famous quote of former Toyota chairman, Eiji Toyoda; and "making people" is certainly a priority for Japanese companies.

Companies like Toyota became renowned for following such an approach. The world-famous Toyota Production System follows the principles of Monozukuri, which revolves around the spirit of not only producing excellent products, but also the ability to constantly improve the production system and processes. Japanese manufacturers both large and small have adopted these principles of Monozukuri, which has helped to set them apart from their competitors when it comes to quality.

Japanese corporations make a lot of efforts in customizing their products to fit to their customers' needs."This involves immense training of new joiners explaining them about company's value systems and teaching them for taking pride in their product creation and uniqueness. This is the essence of Monozukari so effectively followed by Toyota.

Japanese multinationals, including Toyota have now training programmes which often involves the training of staff in factories and subsidiaries overseas. These companies ensure that the values of Monozukuri and high-quality standards are adopted by their workers abroad.

Keeping customers in focus always, Toyota develops long term strategies and then invests in people and technology with an exceptional speed. They dislike any short term measures which do not ensure growth of the organisation. Knowing well that customers will always want more, Toyota's business models and practices are ahead of customers' expectations. In fact their well-managed continuous improvement plans take care of ever growing customers aspirations.

# –4–

# PROBLEMS OF INDIA

## 4.1 What Do You Mean By 'Indian Quality'?

In foreign countries like Japan, and sometimes even in India, the phrase 'Indian quality' is often used. In some cases, a few cheap products of low quality could tarnish the image of Indian exports. Cheap labor is one of the factors that made China a success as the 'factory of the world'. India has the huge challenge of using cheap labor for producing better quality products through a massive skill development program. Before this, we have seen in Bangladesh that how pursuing only cheaper labor may bring about a tragedy. On 24th April 2013, an eight-storied commercial building named Rana Plaza collapsed in the Savar Upazila of Dhaka, Bangladesh. It is considered to be the deadliest garment factory accident in history, with a death toll of about 1,129. It is very dangerous to think that low quality can be allowed in India, just because there are customers who may be willing to buy lower-priced products.

Also, it may look like a selfish way of thinking of the developed countries. These countries have a developed economy, use automation and efficiency improvement for cost reduction. It may be another matter that in some situations and times an easier way also could reduce costs. Getting the same work done in low-wage foreign countries reduces costs. Semiconductor manufacturers shifted the process of manufacturing silicon substrate to Southeast Asia in the distant past. The United States also has a system called 'maquiladora,' under which the only assembling processes were being done in Mexico for low wages. This low wage caused China to become the so-called factory of the world. However, we don't think this way of thinking is correct. Although the distance between San Diego in the United States and Tijuana in Mexico is less than 100 km, different pay for the same work would not become a long-lasting business formula.

We should use the words 'Indian quality' to indicate the excellence of the quality of products made in India. We must not provide products and services of inadequate or unreliable quality to the customers. Customers will never come back again, in such a case. Once we truly provide a product of good quality, we may receive a higher reward. On the contrary, we should learn to accept a lesser reward when the quality is not up to the mark. We can request or expect higher rewards with better quality.

Then what should we do so that the world comes to admit that Indian quality is good quality?' Some of the answers lie in studying the techniques for quality assurance and managing efficiency improvements that are practiced around the world. But there may be a lot of Indian managers lamenting that no results are being achieved by introducing the foreign management systems. They should consider the possibility that they may have acquired only a superficial knowledge of the systems.

**Disaster of Rana Plaza Collapse**

## 4.2 Rupee

In 2007, there was a big buzz about India in Japan. There were a lot of books on the potential of India. At that time, Japanese broadcast stations made special programs on India. They reported on the vibrant Indian industries, the rise of the IT industry, the stable growth of the automobile giant Maruti Suzuki, the healthcare industry and so on. The evaluation of the rupee in November 2007 was Rs. 40 per dollar and 2.72 yen per rupee. Most had predicted that the rupee would rise in value.

Every country in the world suffered the effects of the economic crisis arising from the Lehman shock. Selling Dollar and the Euro for risk avoidance caused the value of the Japanese yen to increase. Japan suffered from stagnant exports. The phenomenon in the Japanese market was special in the way that the stock prices were low, but the currency value was high. Furthermore, Japan was hit by a gigantic earthquake in the eastern part. The Shinzo Abe government of Japan, which assumed power on 26$^{th}$ December 2012, tried to rectify the situation by taking concrete measures to counter the spiral of deflation that Japan has been suffering for the last 10 years or more. Japan has barely recovered from the deflation and is still suffering from its recession.

Now the growth rate of the economy of India has overtaken China's. In spite of India's impressive growth, rupee evaluation is at the lowest. The foreign currency reserve that India has is hardly increasing. Too much of appreciation of the currency like Japanese yen is not always welcomed, but normally, an increase in the currency valuation symbolizes a stronger economy. The situation in India is the opposite of this. Depreciation of rupee means a lack of the attractiveness of the economy. What do you have to do in order to increase the attractiveness of the economy? A suggestion is that you adopt a different thinking in order to make India's business as solid as a rock.

One can find many guidebooks on advancing India's prospects in Japan. Every book talks about the problems faced by Japanese companies that venture into India, which are related to the infrastructure and education in India. This is very understandable as developed countries have experienced the same. Now let us focus on education. As a matter of fact, the Government of India may even be aware of it. The education we refer to here is not about the nuances in the field of sciences but simply about the way of thinking. This education is not the kind that is imparted in schools, yet it can be done at any place like at home, in the office or in the community.

## 4.3 The Quality of Indian Products and Services

### 4.3.1 A Devil Is Living in the Apartment

Now let us try to understand the experiences of a Japanese business person who came to live in India. He moved into an apartment house to start his life in India. Right from the first night, something or the other kept breaking down every day. One thing after another bothered him. There were problems in electrical devices: lamps, geysers, circuit breakers and extension cords, and no right fitting furniture too. One night, the power was down in his room while lights were still working in others. The circuit breaker of his room was functioning. He exclaimed in utter shock, "What is happening? My room is all in the dark and I can't speak Hindi." Finally, he found the burnt main circuit breaker of his room in the basement of the building. Another night, the gorgeous lights hanging in the living room suddenly dropped silently to the floor. He was lucky for not being injured. He even started wondering if a devil was living in his apartment.

When we visit a high-class hotel or restaurant, we can expect a warm-hearted service in India. But these places are very expensive and very few in number. Services provided in the country's railways, road transport, government hospitals, golf courses and so on seem to be generally insufficient or unsatisfactory compared to global standards. The greetings and manners are not refined enough, explanations are unclear and no advance information is provided. These kinds of services can never satisfy global customers. It is a matter of severe concern and many may just decide that they don't want these products or services from India. At the same time, in healthcare and medical tourism there are indications of services being appreciated.

We might think that the essence of the problem is that people do not yet realize what such situations mean in the global context. Indians have been, in the past, existing in an environment where they did not have to fight strongly for survival in a socialist society, and therefore, they are not accustomed to severe competition. Such a person may easily declare that he could do it but would actually give up once he faces the hardship that the task involves. He may say he would gradually learn but would never be able to deliver what he promised. So, he has to find a way to compete in the global market.

**A Devil in the House**

## 4.3.2 One Should Understand and Learn about the World Instead of Thinking about Just Oneself

We think people should study the quality level of India's products and services better, and compare it to the global standards. If we want to improve quality, we should investigate by asking questions to foreigners, not just the local people. Adopting an attitude that it is okay to neglect and not put oneself into the customers' shoes and always thinking only about self-satisfaction would naturally lead to poor quality products and heartless services.

The basic problem is that one may not realize this situation to be bad enough if one cares only about oneself in India. Self-satisfaction cannot help in improving anything or give someone the ability to identify problems. Therefore, technological improvements cannot be expected in such situations. We think this issue should be studied thoroughly and considered as the key problem.

We may not need to compete for survival in the global market because we may have sufficient food. We may be able to keep on walking as before. But this can't help us overtake China or eliminate poverty from Indian society. When we want to compete in the true sense, all Indians have to be aware of the good quality of the products and services in the world. In order to do that, we think leaders of India's industries firstly need an awareness revolution.

**Awareness Revolution**

## 4.3.3 Importance and Difficulty of Awareness Revolution

The importance of an awareness revolution has been understood by a lot of enterprises. Many enterprises, especially the excellent ones, plan regular education programs for new as well as experienced employees.

They train and develop each employee as a person, at the same time educating him about technical matters. The awareness revolution basically means that ideas should be changed, and the past ones thrown away. It looks like the best way to switch to a tidy life for a person who has led a sloppier life until now. In short, it is necessary to start from the acceptance that "I need to change from the past." There may be many who are skeptical about the same. They may even claim to be aware. Many people tend take the serious matter easy. The education of employees toward an awareness revolution is difficult in Japan too. Reformation is doing something that has never been done in the past. It is easy for a man to accept something when he is not required to make an effort. For instance, when a new product is put on the market, a person buys the product to try it on his body. However, when it is necessary to change his or her usual behavior and way of thinking, there is always resistance. There is a phrase called 'three-day monk' in Japan. It refers to a person who has no perseverance. Despite having decided to start doing something good every day, in his mind, he can't continue for more than three days. Considerable amount of will power is necessary do it alone, whereas the coach and the teacher are good guides. Words and actions of coaches are generally considered as rules in a company; they play an important part in awareness revolution in excellent companies. Performance of coaches goes a long way to exploit the full potential of employees and keeps them in high morale.

Among the several manufacturing companies, only a few may have implemented the awareness revolution. Those are the enterprises making the most effort in the world. The managers of enterprises need to learn more about awareness revolution. A human being is basically conservative. It's difficult for him or her to break away from their past routine. Whether it can be done or not becomes the key to success. The words 'Indian quality' should become synonymous with 'wonderful quality.' In order to realize this, one should analyze what went wrong and think of methods to change it. This is the job of the top management. It is not the job of the person in-charge or the worker.

*"Having no problem is the biggest problem of all"*

Taiichi Ohno
**Founder Toyota Production System**

*"The best approach is to dig out and eliminate problems where they are assumed not to exist"*

**Shigeo Shingo**

# –5–

# GOOD POINTS OF INDIA

## 5.1 Rich Population is Good

We all know India has a large population. At the same time, the one-child policy of China has created a distorted population and age structure. This means it needs to take countermeasures for taking care of the disadvantages caused due to the imbalance. But India too has the problem of income disparity when compared to China. The structure of age-wise distribution of population in India is a beautiful favorable pyramid though.

It is also estimated that, between 2015 and 2030, India's urban population will rise to nearly 600 million people.

This means that India is more comfortable in terms of availability of adequate workforce until a far future, and has a brighter future. It is understandable that it follows socialist ideas to ensure food for everybody. Human beings should always work diligently, honoring ancestors, experience a good childhood, develop into good citizens and contribute to the overall growth of society and country. We should fulfil our responsibility to raise our children in such a manner that they face any global challenge maintaining family bondages. This should be a universal code, regardless of religion, ethnicity and country. That way, isn't India a big power owing to its large population and family-oriented society?

## 5.2 The Indian Is Expected

Recently, the improvement in quality of services in some public institutions, especially in airports, is remarkable, thanks to the effort and support of the Government of India. The rush at the check-in counters has almost disappeared. Waiting rooms are being kept clean, and the uniform of housekeepers has been changed to a more stylish and attractive attire. Cabin crew members are collecting trash with the cooperation of passengers in the low-cost carriers, just before landing. This is to ensure that the next flight departs on schedule, with the realization that messy situations cause delay. Also, in the process, the airline doesn't have to bother to hire extra housekeepers either.

Although this is gradual, this is certainly an improvement. First of all, as mentioned earlier, we need to learn what good quality and service means. This is the kind of game where the one who is the most learned will win against the other. A customer might feel unhappy with the defective products sold to him. But is the only problem here that the customer feels sad? Is it okay to be so? A customer might face troubles and become unhappy over poor service and bad manners. What kind of professional would one be if he remains calm or indifferent, claiming that logically it was not his fault? Shouldn't one's customers be treated better than their own family? Shouldn't one regard a customer as a new-born baby? One will sacrifice anything for their baby and take precautions to protect him or her from impending dangers. This is the human instinct. There will be a big difference when we apply it to our business.

However, we had better consider the fact that people also have a devil inside of them. When one starts something with the question "Should I even do these kinds of things?" it is troublesome. The devil inside our mind doesn't allow us to be a hard worker. However, we should think it over. People in India have the ability. There are 38 world heritage sites in India ranking it the sixth in the list. Several Indians have won the Nobel

Prize. Yes, an Indian surely has the ability. Yet only 40 million people in a population of more than 1.3 billion people are paying the income tax. Furthermore, half of them are civil servants and pensioners. India should enable more Indians citizens to pay the income tax, giving them a chance to use their abilities.

Recent changes are bringing more individuals into the tax net and improved economic activities. However, with several tax exemptions and other populist schemes coming up regularly, not much is expected to change.

> **IT+IT=IT**
> **INDIAN TALENT+INFORMATION TECHNOLOGY= INDIA TOMORROW**
> Prime Minister: Narendra Modi

# –6–

# Why Do Quality Problems Occur in India?

The perception of Indian quality is also related to our way of thinking. So let's analyze this background first.

## 6.1 Mild Climate and Abundant Food

Unlike Japan, India is a multi-ethnic country. Many languages are spoken here and as many as 17 languages feature in their currency bills. However, there are more than 200 dialects in India. India has no unified national language though Hindi is the most used. To any foreigner, a country without a national language is unusual. We know that English is like a common language in India. Many Japanese people seem to be under the impression that almost all Indians can handle English, but actually very few among the Indian population speak English like a native speaker. Usually, the local language is used for communication or English is used as a secondary language.

The fundamentals of any culture are in their religion, language and so on. The favorable environment in the Indian sub-continent allowed humans to select from the abundantly available food and natural resources. History and nature too might have contributed to the DNA of the Indian people. There are a large number of Indians who are very industrious, attentive to others and creative in their ideas, and many of them are now heading global companies; more such examples are required. India will prosper if they have more such diligent people. We need to think about the competitive future in the world market and work toward being more diligent, attentive, creative and original. After all, it was an Indian who discovered the 'zero.'

## 6.2 The Gods Might Be Angry

Almost all companies in India, with the exception of a few, may have heard of the '5Ss.' A lot of posters on 5S are displayed in the workplaces of most Indian organizations. But the posters are sometimes too dirty to read what is written. Near the workplaces you often find trash scattered and components to be assembled stacked chaotically. One can spot seemingly defective pieces lying here and there. There are two types of defects: one where products with defects are tagged, but no dates are shown. The other type is when seemingly defective products are found lying hidden in invisible places. The workplace might seem like the best place to hide defective and non-usable items for them. The posters of 5S look very sad too. It is a well-known fact that the 5S is the foundation for all improvement efforts in any organization or society.

Why does such a situation exist in such a company that is trying to introduce a management method like JIT, TPM, TQM or 6 Sigma? The causes may be quite deep-rooted. It may be owing to the environment that they have grown up in.

Almost everyone in India believes in the existence of God. We speak or listen to God. On the other hand, Japanese youngsters hardly believe in the existence of God. Japanese people do not pray every day like Indians do. When young people in Japan get married, they may go to the Shinto Shrine for eternal love. And when they die, the Buddhist temple takes care of the last rituals. People in India might consider the Japanese to be groundless and negligent. Yet in Japan, you hardly see any chaos at the traffic intersection even without any signals. After the tsunami disaster in 2011, they waited patiently in the queue for drinking water even when it took more than two hours. Nobody sneaked into the front of the line. In India, quite a lot of drivers go the wrong way and neglect signals. What are they praying for, to their Gods every morning? Are the Gods allowing us to behave this way? It is not surprising that India loses almost 200,000 young people every year in traffic related accidents.

A foreigner may think that people in India don't feel the need to observe the rules in public. One can also see such behavior in the society here. People may have a typical way of thinking that as everybody breaks the rules, they too are not required to follow them.

But we have to understand that any management method without exception cannot bear fruits until all employees observe the rules. We cannot expect any results when almost everyone disregards the rules. If traffic rules are disregarded by individuals (occasionally even the policemen break the rule), then order cannot be maintained. Any effective method becomes irrelevant without adhering to the rules. No wonder a Japanese consultant once said, "I am afraid that the God in India will be really angry." No management within the organizations can improve adherence to rules and standards, if the employees do not respect the rules in the society they live. This is the real problem for India to become world class.

## 6.3 No Pain, No Gain

When an Indian company introduces an efficiency improvement method, the top management usually misunderstands that the expert consultants would change the culture of the company without their involvement. Introducing a new method to the company means changing the culture, which is extremely hard and difficult—just like changing the blood type of human beings. In order to do this, the top management has to take positive and voluntary action as per the advice of the consultant. Many people here are reluctant to adopt a 'Gemba' culture, which requires visiting the actual site or scene of work. They like to discuss and settle the matter in the meeting room. They are not aware of the possibility of incorrect information being shared, misleading and affecting one's judgment on an important issue. There are rules about effective quality control methods. Management should use the data that is reliably collected in a regulated or planned manner to take the right decision. A check sheet makes sense only if all parameters are checked faithfully as stipulated.

In order to introduce quality control and efficiency improvement techniques, users should be qualified to use them. You cannot let people use guns, without the knowledge of their dangers and operation. The reason why many companies in Japan and other industrialized countries have succeeded in using these kinds of methods is that they have accepted the problems in their way of functioning and have followed rules obediently. Many Indian companies should consider this matter seriously.

The change of culture in the whole organization can't be achieved until the top management of the companies reflects on the past and makes an effort to create a new culture for the employees. The top management's attitude is of great importance if the company wants to compete in the global market.

**No Pain No Gain**

# –7–

# WHAT MAKE THINGS DIFFICULT TO SUCCEED?

## 7.1 The Problems in the Indian Manufacturing Sector

India is a large and diverse nation with a population of 1.3 plus billion people, sixth in world economy with almost 2.8 trillion US dollars in GDP. With more than a million people joining the job market every month, there cannot be a better time for India to engage all its resources and eliminate poverty once and for all.

Historically, the manufacturing sector has not contributed enough (only 16%) to the economy. However, it is clear that this untapped potential must be exploited to achieve global standards.

During the past decade, the Indian economy focused on services rather than manufacturing. The Indian manufacturing industry was stagnant for many years and showed a negative growth in the financial year 2013–2014. Because of this, in 2014, the Indian prime minister launched the 'Make in India' campaign. The aim of the campaign is to transform India into a global design and manufacturing hub. In pursuit of this, India is focusing on the development of its infrastructure, increasing and tailoring its talent pool to the needs of the manufacturing industry, attracting investment through aggressive FDI initiatives, and by increasing the ease of doing business through legal and tax reforms.

India has a large pool of talented engineers and managers, abundant supply of labor at a low cost and a huge domestic demand for manufactured goods. It is surprising that even with so many positive factors, we have not been able to take advantage and grow our economy to an acceptable level.

It is evident that our education system and skill development plans did not produce desirable results, with a few exceptions. There is an urgent need to understand our own cultural background, learn from examples of global and domestic excellence in businesses and integrate all our resources to become a lean, efficient and quality-oriented country.

Manufacturing labor is very cheap in India, even when compared to China. In 2018, the average cost of manufacturing labor per hour was $2.0 in India and $4.5 in China. While this cost seems much lower, one has to take into account the extra costs incurred due to India's significantly worse and more expensive transportation, power and water costs. Also losses due to, red-tapism, corruption, political interference and unions should be considered.

These issues ensure that India does not become the preferred destination for manufacturing. India has a huge labor force (of nearly 500 million people,) including unskilled workers and a rich talent pool of skilled workers, such as researchers and engineers who are capable of lending cost-effective research and development support to manufacturing operations. Last year, the *Wall Street Journal* reported that 12 million people enter the Indian labor market each year. Furthermore, India has the second largest English-speaking population in the world, behind the US, of course. Most large Indian factories produce high-quality goods because they use high-quality equipment and tools, and they take pride in their work. Many Indian factories are family-run and well-known for the care and transparency of their work and business dealings. Unlike China, India does not carry the stigma of poor-quality production.

However, small and medium-size companies still depend a lot on segregation, rework and inspection rather than avoiding defects and wastes all over. About 80% of India's manufacturing manpower work in such organizations. Lack of understanding and application is the main cause of continuing with an old way of working. Many multinational companies in India have been able to overcome such difficulties by massive cultural and transformational changes, to measure up to global excellence standards. The growth of the automotive sector and its export from India is an example of a success story.

## 7.2 Historic Issues

We know the effects of historical, regional and locational issues in India. Being a country with masses practicing different cultures and lifestyles in different regions has contributed to the way people here think and behave. There are some human attributes that make things rather complex if not very difficult. The aspiration of the different human workforces, those in blue collar jobs and managers, are different. And at times, it is challenge for a company to educate a diverse group of people belonging to localized groups and sets, about the company culture. It results in company policies and education getting diluted as individual efforts are not as effective.

There are differences in the perception of people belonging to such diverse educational backgrounds. A large part of the workforce for the industry may come from rural backgrounds and many may have no formal schooling, training or skills. The industry has traditionally been driven by public sectors which may have imparted some basic skills to the workforce, just enough to complete their jobs. Such a workforce may at times be subjected to social exploitation. This has resulted in regions where workers formed unions. We know the typical political situations in several states, resulting into labor unions not even sparing Japanese industries in India. Unrest in Suzuki, Honda and Toyota establishments did not go well with Japanese investors. At the same time, real growth and development of workforce suffered.

Workforce from large agriculture-oriented societies has had to depend on nature. Over the years, young villagers moved to industrial towns seeking jobs, leaving their abject conditions, which could not provide education, power and sanitation. This force also needs to be trained and it necessitates time and concerted efforts from the industry, the education sector, and the government—to provide basic amenities for these workers to grow as a capable workforce. These classes do not move from one place to another and they continue with their jobs in their respective areas.

On the other hand, the manager class has the benefit of education and could move from one job to another to achieve their goals and provide for their families' growth.

Typically, such managers will change their jobs and take up new assignments. Thus, the management may not impart continued skill training for their workers and staff, resulting in lack of motivation among the workforce. Such a manager working either in a Japanese or any global environment, might be a better engineer or manager thanks to continuous learning.

Somewhere these factors have resulted in insufficient infrastructure and investments for training and improvement. The resource crunch and the existing decision-making process have contributed to a lack of focus on management. Ad hoc investments without long-term plans have impacted the outcome in such industries. Though the industries are growing, they may not live up to the expectations. The result is that the hard work put in by the management, managers and workers remain unsynchronized and do not achieve any common goals.

## 7.3 Protected Industry

The industry has also been protected by various policies of government, which keep the inefficient and low-quality production going, to foster the employment rate. The concerns regarding the existing industries stem from such factors. The protection offered by the policies and low growth and volume have lowered the necessity and motivation for setting best practices standards. The industries that did not upgrade have had to face the severe burden of change (e.g. like Ambassador cars in the auto industry.)

## 7.4 Way of Thinking

For the sake of this book, let us restrict ourselves to the typical way of thinking of employees here. This may not be very accurate as a general rule.

But we may agree that a large part conscious or subconscious thinking is similar, resulting in the general behavior.

We know that due to many disparities and regional issues, most of the employees only want to grow for themselves. This is the primary factor restraining one from putting in enough efforts, as they feel there are no growth opportunities for them. If they are not doing well, then they would change the job.

Many a times due to such individual behavior, a person is not aligned to the company. The top management's directions do not get percolated downwards to the juniors and their teams.

People here are ready to ask many questions to the extent of being argumentative at times. But they do not implement the decisions wholeheartedly.

In the Japanese society, for instance, juniors are expected to provide their ideas and plans and explain the same to their teams and bosses. Once a decision is taken, the whole team joins in to implement it wholeheartedly. Respect for seniors, working as a team and having regular brainstorming for problem solving are typical Japanese behaviors, which result in strong customer-focused organizations.

No individual wants to be held responsible for failure or non-conformity. These cultural factors ensure that the root cause analysis remains feeble and ineffective.

In other words, people just pass the blame. This reminds us of one of the conversations that a person from India had with his Japanese guest. While it is easy to feel proud about the heritage of India and pass on the blame to years of colonial rule, how does one explain habits like spitting *pan masala* on streets and buildings? Or people driving their vehicle on the wrong side of the road, jumping a traffic signal, leading to chaos and more traffic jams? A person who violates traffic rules creates a mess. And this cannot be blamed on acquired traits or habits.

Look at Japan. In 1945, Hiroshima and Nagasaki—almost half of the country—were completely destroyed. But within 20 years, the citizens took responsibility and developed the nation.

**Unless we stop blaming others, gear up to become disciplined, and respect our nation, rules and our surroundings, we cannot improve. And this change should come from within us.**

## 7.5 Consumer Attitude

In many ways, the consumer attitude has been defined by such products in the market. An attitude of accepting anything, even when it is not up to high standards, has gripped us.

A typical example of this consumer behavior encouraging poor quality is the after-market sales of auto industry components. Manufacturers in the auto industry are mostly Japanese and European companies and their products measure up to international standards. However, the consumer behavior is to compromise on service and maintenance by using low-cost after-market products. The consumer behavior is to save money in the short-term by not insisting on genuine spare parts. This contributes to low-cost and poor-quality products finding acceptability.

The consumer is now getting more safety conscious. An example is that airbags are again becoming popular in cars. Earlier, makers did not provide airbags as these added to the costs.

Also, the consumer maturity in India needs to change. Consumers here like to maintain and somehow keep the product functioning even after its expected lifespan, instead of going for updated and better-quality products. Such ways of thinking in India are also undergoing a rapid change now.

Interestingly, consumers are becoming increasingly aware and want to avoid cheap products like the ones imported from China. Many distributors think that importing cheap products from China can help them make money quickly. However, consumers are tending to avoid such products.

Manufacturers often try to take refuge in the consumer behavior of buying cheapest products compromising on quality. Some management may think that quality maintenance is additional expenditure, which the consumers may not pay for. However, such products end up being rejected by the consumer over a period of time.

## 7.6 How to Improve the Situation?

We need to understand why some of the Indian produces have the highest quality, meeting global standards. Software made in India and auto industry support systems for exporting cars and two-wheelers have been trying to achieve the best global standards. Also, to an extent, the garment sector may be one of the few exceptions. However, even these industries do need to make continuous improvements to sustain their advantages in the future.

To achieve real growth, we have to fundamentally improve the quality of the goods and services from India.

The company management needs to realize and agree that better quality stuff makes better business sense too. Increasing the importance of security and safety and adhering to the environmental standards required for their products and services will set the companies and brands apart from the poor-quality ones. At the same time, government agencies must understand that no unfair trade practices in this approach will be rewarding.

However, the most important and contextual issue here is for industries to set a voluntary standard. The adherence to standards set by themselves will be difficult and challenging. The principles for continuous improvement as outlined in these chapters are some of the tools that the management can use, self-regulate and adhere to, in their companies. Unless the company and its employees strive to better themselves, the company may fail in its objectives of reaching its target.

Many companies in different states of India have done extremely well in achieving global excellence levels of efficiency, productivity and quality. There are several examples of Deming Prize winners that speak very highly of talented engineers and managers who have worked diligently and trained their labor force to follow best practices.

Achieving business excellence within the organization purely depends on the leadership's understanding of the issues and hard work meeting the aspirations of people, thus procuring positive results, meeting global standards. However, taking it further, the entire supply chain needs to be supportive of the improvement, as it is also plagued by similar problems.

Most of the young Indians in the labor force come from a village background and they need to be molded and trained before they are expected to deliver good quality output. Comprehensive understanding of hygiene, safety, quality, productivity and customer satisfaction is a must over the years, in developing a strong and committed labor force.

It is important to have a good understanding of the Indian law and rights of workers so that unions are better handled and trained manpower does not get misguided, which is still common in India.

## 7.7 Why Don't We Return to the Basics in the Long Run?

This is one of the discussions in a brainstorming session between an Indian entrepreneur and a Japanese consultant on ways to help the situation in India. The consultant looks at this as a typical example of going back to basics.

An Indian entrepreneur is running a start-up impacting rural life and helping employment generation in tribal areas by providing technological solutions to silk yarn producers—introducing solar-run yarn and weaving machines. His customers are mostly state government organizations, which endeavor to help social causes. The condition of government-procured raw material is abysmal and the quality is minimal.

However, this entrepreneur is keen on effecting a change by not imposing it, but by motivating employees to adopt change as a tool to better the lives of employees and customers, thus making an impact on the customers.

He conducted a survey of his employees to check what gives them the most happiness. Several managers also came up with ideas on improving their working and employment conditions, which were also appreciated. However, one employee had an answer that needs a mention in the context of this book.

He said that he got happiness from making his customer happy. This is a simple and basics fact that will shower greater satisfaction for employees in their jobs. Around the same time, this company also received many complaints from customers. So, he organized his service teams to visit all the customer locations and check out the reasons behind the complaints. To his surprise, he found that all his customers had placed their machines in unused storage spaces and unhygienic environments. Some customers were not even taking proper care of the simple machines. As a result, the machines had excessive wear and tear.

Now to come to the key point: The management had decided that its motto was to make customers happy. So what could it do instead of just passing blame on to customers? The management invested in spares and got all the machines running. Customers were trained in the upkeep of the machines. This simple effort made the customers happy and ensured repeat orders. It is important to always think of others.

It all comes down to how the employees need to experience the quality and motivation to deliver the same quality to leave their clients satisfied. The first mantra is to make and adopt the change to be a better person in your life and appreciate a better way of living and delivering.

Most people here follow many principles in life. We follow many sages and saints who have over the years given us treasures of advice on how to improve our lives. Contributing to the society and people in need is a way of life in India. Live in harmony with nature and worship and respect nature. Keep the environment clean, where gods can be worshiped. These are in fact the simple principles of 5S or quality improvement techniques that the Japanese consultant was trying to explain. We have had it in us for centuries and ages; so why not follow these basic principles in our jobs?

## 7.8 It Is Good to Learn

There are several methods by which the manufacturing industries try to enhance quality and reduce cost. Each manufacturing company adopts one for corporate quality duly certified through an auditing authority. Awards like the Deming Prize may be one such certification of corporate quality. There are lots of quality management activities, systems or practices. TQM, 6 Sigma, and TS/ISO series of standards on quality are also popular in India. There are some Indian companies that invite consultants from Japan to undertake productivity improvement. Several Japanese TPM consultants are working in India and showing impressive results.

There is a long-term program called the Visionary Leaders for Manufacturing (VLFM) program for India's manufacturing executives conducted by JICA (Japan International Cooperation Agency). Many progressive-minded companies of India join in and get results. There is also another system called AOTS-Program supported by the Japanese government. Indian companies can apply and send their staff to study in Japan as part of this program. In addition, Japan set up two centers in India for training and it plans to grant work visa for 200,000 skilled Indian people to work in Japan. These platforms help India's business runners, managers and would-be managers to study the management system in Japan. Apart from this, many Indian companies conduct training sessions or invite consultants over to improve production efficiency. Despite the learning, one sees quite a different world in the actual workplace. There are a few companies that have benefited through such deployments. Most others hardly bear any fruits. It is good to learn, but it is meaningless if things learned are not practiced—so there are no results.

Foreign companies like the Japan-based ones are introducing their own management methods, at times forcefully, to sustain quality levels. But many such companies are also suffering due to the high expense of bringing representatives from mother countries like Japan, Europe or USA, and equipment depreciation. We are not at all pleased at the general impression that we acquire the mettle for global competitiveness only with the help of foreign companies.

As Indians, we have to take charge or responsibility to change ourselves and our colleagues and be proud of our products and services in the world. We have to kick-start an awareness revolution here. As a foreigner who has lived in India, my impression is that when an Indian says "I know", it is almost always only on the surface. He or she hardly ever means it. The person has never seen any Indian origin company using the management method in the true meaning. In Japan, even at the worker level, people are skilled for data analysis and problem solving, while we see them rarely even in supervisors at manufacturing industries here. Simply put, most of the business runners who studied the theory and got a driving license often break traffic rules and can't drive safely.

## 7.9 We Need More Practice

According to articles in Japanese newspapers, in 2006, the rupee was expected to rise up thanks to the expansion of export, supported by the explosive growth of the IT industry, their English-speaking skills and the smartness of Indians. But now, the growth rate of IT industry is slowing down. The trade deficit is being felt and the value of the rupee is more than 50 percent down against the US$ as compared to 2006. Although everyone in the world, not just the Indians, kept a tab, the Indian economy could hardly accelerate.

Why don't we discuss the causes that made things difficult at that point? When a human being grows in a good environment, he doesn't need to always think of the daily occurrences and possibilities. Unless he is trained to think and generate ideas every day, he can hardly take appropriate action. He may secure an unexpected result because of this. However, someone who is not well-trained will imagine that the reason was the unexpected result of others' action and not his. We had better throw away this habit of making excuses.

It is assumed that one has a purpose. It maybe one's duty. For instance, one has to gather in the conference room at nine o'clock because there is a conference scheduled at that time. He has to make his remarks clearly because it is an important meeting. It is necessary to think about the elements that caused a failure and possible ways to succeed as well. The traffic jam in the morning may have been more awful that day. The alarm clock might not have worked because of dead batteries. There may be lots more. The technique for analyzing a failure mode and taking steps to correct the situation is called Failure Mode Effect Analysis (FMEA). It is a technique adopted by the quality control, but do we take the recommended corrective action? FMEA is a technique to find the possibility of failures and prevent them from achieving the purpose without any further hiccups. This corresponds to the arrangement of 1S of 5S. It means adopting a nice and beautiful logic. We believe we have the ability to act as per FMEA. However, there are quite a lot of people who don't take FMEA seriously. Why aren't they serious? What if someone from a military organization summoned you to attend a nine o'clock meeting for a discussion? Going late and being poor at the discussion would have consequences. Everyone would desperately execute the FMEA out of fear. This is an awareness revolution propelled by fear. Most of us don't respond seriously in an ordinary scenario because we think it's permissible to be late and we could get away with our verbal skills instead of doing the homework or by just muttering an excuse. One becomes serious out of fear of not being able to reach the airport to catch a flight on time and hence becomes prompt in such situations. The Japanese feel guilty about causing trouble for others; so, in their case, the FMEA is adhered to automatically due to their strong will to never fall behind schedule.

Each individual can say whatever he wants in the world's largest democratic country, unlike in China where people have to compulsorily take directions. To phrase it differently, an individual is always thinking of himself and it is very difficult for him to think seriously about customer satisfaction. We may have to consider the fact that such negative personality traits may cause greater danger. This has decreased the competitive edge of the products and services in India. Training is necessary so that he always views things from a customer's standpoint instead of just thinking about himself.

People around the world think India can lead the world economy in future. Someday, India will be relied on by people all over the world. Lately, engineers and managers in India are upgrading their skills to be better team players and contribute toward integrating the efforts of organization. It has been observed that a good quality leader in a company is able to motivate his people by identifying their strengths and weaknesses and deploying them toward the purpose and objectives of his company. The current situation of India needs to be improved to realize the goals in future. We have to change our awareness to correct our wrong aspects while improving upon the good ones.

# –8–

# What Should Be Learned from Toyota?

## 8.1 The First Is Human Resources

Now we will study Toyota, which is one of the greatest enterprises in the world. As we mentioned earlier, excellent companies understand well that it is people who make an enterprise. It is always men who make machines, design, buy parts, sell products, and maintain lines. It is men who make goods according to the standards, and it is also the same men who make defective ones. Excellent companies in the world, including Toyota, take efforts to educate employees, without exception. The more the number of professional employees the enterprise has, the better machines it will have, the lesser defects it will see, leading to a higher productivity ratio. Profit goes up and the employees' rewards increase. It will depend on the ability of a true manager to generate this virtuous circle. However, great efforts are needed to reach there.

The Toyota Company established a work culture called the 'Toyota Way', which was a set of business principles. It was based on the kaizen principle of continuous improvement, which strives to eliminate waste and overproduction as well as create a system wherein any employee can suggest a change when they see it fit. There is a high premium on human participation. There is constant encouragement for further innovation, consensus and ideas for continuous improvement. The Toyota Way also focuses on long-term improvement rather than just the short-term one. The two main pillars of the Toyota Way are 'customer first' and 'respect for people'.

Enterprises that fail to become excellent companies may think that education could be wasteful because an employee may resign after he is educated. A fool can work with *poka-yoke* (mistake-proofing). *Poka-yoke* is not perfect. The defect doesn't stop because too many elements are related to the human factor. Machine breakdowns happen frequently. Line stoppages can happen anytime. Employees may not feel happy working in the environment, and may be less productive. Every person working in the company must be professional, without any exception. That is why employees receive compensation. The professional takes pride and also boasts about his work. He will never deliver defective goods to a customer. The competence of an enterprise is proportional to the number of professionals among all people (the subcontractors included) vis-a-vis the operations. The business administrator should consider if the work he is assigning could be handled professionally by employees or not. It seems that the system at Toyota is making the most of this aspect. Excellent companies have respect for their people

**Respect for People Makes a Great Organization**

## 8.2 The Importance of Basics

If the products and services churned out in India are excellent, more customers at home and abroad would prefer to buy Indian products. Excellent products and services with better market acceptance will generate the passion required to come out with improved products to counter competition. Better products and services would lead to an increase in domestic and foreign consumption. When the industry is activated, Indian's purchasing ability would also increase and help the GDP increase.

The quality of Indian products and services may be linked to the vulnerability of economy. If we expect economic development only due to natural advantages like population and availability of abundant resources, we may be overtaken by other competitors among the emerging nations. If we think extremely low labor costs is enough, we may not be able to attract the global market. The quality of Indian products and services might be affected by the way of thinking and the characteristics of the people here. India may not be able to become the world leader without an awareness revolution in this matter. Why don't we rethink and start from scratch?

Running is a basic sport. To run well, the lower body should be strengthened firmly. This is the basic acumen required to become a successful sprinter. We can't be skillful with a weak lower body. A weakly-built sportsperson often tries to cheat. In the business world, a businessman who speaks well but can't keep the promise is comparable to this nature and attitude. He will end up delivering products or services that are quite different from the presentation he made. He then blames the customer for wrong usage in case of a reported fault in the product he supplied. He is always speaking of customer satisfaction but does not act in accordance. This kind of scenario will plunge India's industry and economy into uncertainty.

What are the bases for strong enterprise management? We only have to research on the actions of great professional men. You will be surprised to find some common answers in unexpected places. You will get to know that the management methods being introduced by many enterprises in recent years are already close at hand. Let's study them.

## 8.3 The Original of All

Consider this extremely simple thing. Nobody prefers lack of cleanliness to cleanliness. Nobody prefers sloppiness over neatness. Cleanliness (*saaf suthra*) and tidiness are the basic qualities that everyone swears by. Nothing is more comprehensible than this. The basic functions in the human world include keeping healthy, studying and developing technologies for better life. Now, take neatness and cleanliness for example. Everyone understands their importance, but not everyone adheres to them. God has kindly made it easy to understand them, but it is difficult to execute them. PDCA and 5S were introduced as a means to help people comprehend such factors. PDCA and 5S are the common senses in manufacturing industries. However, these are not executed easily. There are two reasons for this. One, its true meaning is not understood by everyone. The other is that the devil in their minds tempts people to be lazy. Let me explain the true meaning of PDCA and 5S and how to execute them in this paragraph. The truth is that a dirty and sloppy factory or office can never do a good job. Such a company cannot win the competition. Therefore, PDCA and 5S are the fundamental requirements to compete in the global market. This is only the starting point. A dirty and sloppy enterprise can't even stand on the starting line.

### 8.3.1 Seiri-Seiton

In the global manufacturing world, the term *seiri* translates to 'sorting out' and *seiton* to 'set in order'. Originally in Japanese, the words *seiri* and *seiton* are not normally used separately but used together as *seiri-seiton*. In the past, the top privileged classes in the Japanese society were the Samurai class, much like the *Kshatriya*s in India. Children born in Samurai families are brought up strictly so that they can respond bravely and properly at the time of an attack by enemy. Searching for weapons after the enemy has attacked doesn't make sense. They have to acquire or lay hands on the weapons even in the dark. It is an ultimate training in visual control that's generally inconceivable to us. They learn *seiri-seiton* as their basic duties. They have to keep their belongings clean and neat always so that they can recognize: what, where and how many are there at all times. As a matter of fact, the original *seiri-seiton* includes cleaning. As he always cleans them, he can identify everything just by touching them with his hands.

Let's disassemble the Chinese characters of 整理整頓 (*seiri-seiton*). 整理 *(seiri)* refers to thinking clearly with logic and 整頓 (*seiton*) means organizing steadily, giving it a nice appearance. The Toyota people invented a technique of separating *seiri* and *seiton* for industrial use.

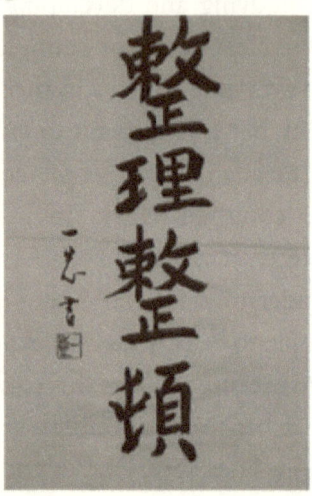

Seiri Seiton

Calligraphy by Hitoshi Tsuneshige
Japanese Calligrapher

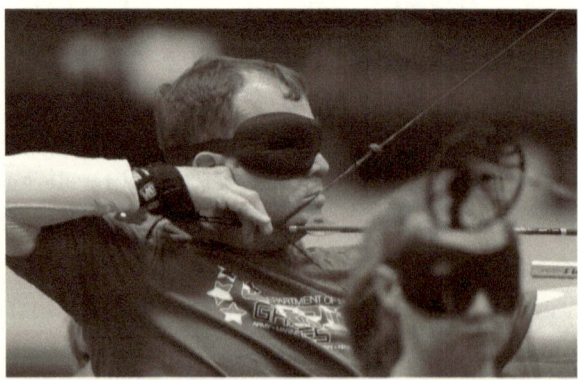

**A Blind Man's Life**

They defined *seiri* as segregating the necessary from the unnecessary logic and *seiton* as a situation wherein you can identify what, where and how many. *Seiri* is like a plan and *seiton* is like action. These definitions are for the people who don't know how to keep their place neat and clean. They are helpful in understanding things. But the important thing is to follow and act according to the definitions. Do most people who claim to know *seiri-seiton* really understand their meanings? A visually handicapped person living nearby would be an expert in *seiri-seiton*. He can't see but knows what, where and how many things he has. He puts a thing only at the designated place and follows the rule faithfully because this is the only way for him to survive. And therefore, he can cook for himself. He can see things with his mind's eyes. As a matter of fact, a man who sees only through his eyes is likely to become sloppy and less productive. Why don't we ponder on this a little more?

## 8.3.2 Seisou

*Seisou* means cleaning, it is very clear. Some translators use 'shine' as it stands for S. According to a Japanese consultant, while visiting an Indian factory, he cannot make out if a housekeeper is cleaning or dirtying up while emptying the trash cans. Managers of the plant are likely to point out that housekeepers are the problem. It wouldn't be convincing. The problem is on the manager's part, isn't it? Housekeepers have been cleaning the same way for a long time without receiving any complaints. They would be at a loss if someone suddenly upbraids them for not getting the place clean enough. They are not at fault. Although some improvements can be seen in the service industry, we have to understand that the cleaning system here is still considerably rudimentary and some even keep dirtying while at the job.

This is a typical situation in India and something that we should reflect on. A manager who claims to know 5Sbut doesn't understand the true meaning of *seisou* can't explain how to improve the cleaning technique and demonstrate it to the housekeepers. Such a manager is not qualified to scold the housekeepers.

*Seisou* is written as 清掃 in Japanese. 清掃 consists of 清 and 掃. 清 (*sei*) means 'to purify,' and 掃 (*sou*) means to 'clean with devices'.

Purifying the workplace is equivalent to facing the gods. Think of how clean we should be for the gods to pay a visit. To clean with devices means employing a high technology for the job. When we purify our workplace, no trace of dust should ever remain. Housekeepers will not get a chance to improve their abilities without managers demonstrating the methods. In its absence, housekeepers will only loaf around on the job and find shortcuts.

Cleaning is an important process in completing the product. Cleaning should be done every day regularly and not just because the place is dirty. It is just like a sportsperson limbering up before practice. Cleaning also includes checking machines, lines, parts, tools and everything, besides purifying the workplace. It is the same as detecting if your lovely child has fever while touching her every day. It corresponds to C of PDCA. A problem can be spotted at once if you check every day and you can take action immediately. Moreover, it will be possible to improve continuously. We should remember that cleaning is a form of engineering. It is needless to say that the technology of the cleaning greatly contributed to the development of the semiconductor and medical treatments. Therefore, we can't win the competition if we consider cleaning as the housekeeper's job alone. Here is a poem through which we can inspire our people to clean our workplace.

*God loves cleanliness,*

*Work is worship, say all wise men.*

*Workplace is a holy place; naturally then*

*Cleaning the workplace makes our God glad.*

*But if it is dirty, He feels so sad,*

*If it is messy, He feels so bad.*

*Clean, clean, clean, clean the workplace everywhere,*

*It is a holy place, 'cause God stays there.*

*For just five minutes clean every day.*

*Keep all dirt and evils away.*

*To keep God happy, that is the way,*

*And we shall be happy and stay that way.*

*Clean, clean, clean is the mantra for success,*

*And God shall be happy and He will bless!*

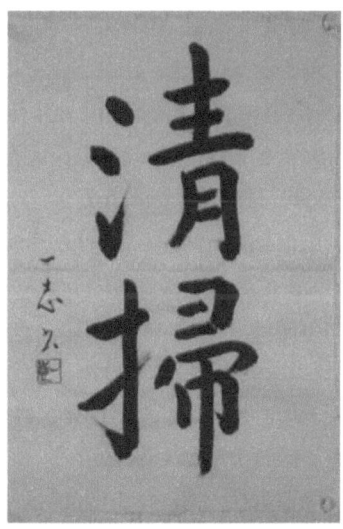

Seisou

Calligraphy by Hitoshi Tsuneshige
Japanese Calligrapher

### 8.3.3 Seiketsu

*Seiketsu* is written as 清潔 in Japanese. A Japanese consultant deems it to be one of the most beautiful Japanese words alongside the following word *shitsuke*. *Seiketsu* is just a term for standardization. It is rather difficult to comprehend the beauty in its meaning or get the results from the implementation of 5S. *Seiketsu* means 'to be pure both physically and mentally'. It refers to general hygiene. Rather than pure, it indicates the absence of any impurity. 清 (*sei*) is like 'clear water.' 潔 (*ketsu*) is like 'the pure mind of an innocent girl'. Therefore, *seiketsu* refers to a perfect state *sans* impurities. In such a state of mind, you will strongly dislike dirt and show the courage to beg for an apology without excuses whenever you are wrong. In order to attain this state, you need to put in a great effort and practise on an everyday basis, especially if you are a leader. It is common sense that subordinates never function well under a bad mouthing and angry leader who shouts orders and instructs them. The fourth 'S' of 5S, *seiketsu*, is defined as implementing the first three 'S's every day repeatedly in TPS. Irregular and intermittent action will not help you achieve *seiketsu*. A visually handicapped person repeats his actions including the first to the third 'S' every day. This is the real 4S, *seiketsu*.

If you simply tell your housekeepers to do the cleaning, without following the three 'S's yourself, you'll not achieve *saiketsu*. If a leader doesn't lead by example, it is useless. Translated into English, *seiketu* means 'training or disciplining for standardization'. As the term *shitsuke* too is mentioned as 'discipline', when translated, it may be confusing at times. As we see in the next paragraph, *shitsuke* doesn't mean discipline.

The top management should impart training and education by scheduling properly. The top management in Indian manufacturing industry should understand that to develop the economy, maintaining cleanliness is much more important than just cleaning. Here is a poem that will inspire them to maintain the cleanliness levels:

*Maintain cleanliness,*

*You keep your place dirty,*

*If you are mean, mean, mean.*

*Then people will tell you to clean, clean, clean,*

*But if you are tidy and keep your place shining,*

*You will also observe that*

*Even the God is smiling.*

*I always love to keep my place clean and neat,*

*And look how my God is happy and sweet.*

*Sometimes the devil enters our heart,*

*And we mess up our workplace,*

*And what a mess we make!*

*And we lose God's grace.*

*But finally God prevails and we learn that it is better*

*To maintain the place clean than*

*Mess up and clean later.*

*Let us take a pledge and take a vow*

*That we shall not dirty the place,*

*From here and now,*

*We shall never litter,*

*And keep dirt and dust away,*

*And use waste bins and baskets,*

*Positively every day.*

*We shall keep our workplace clean ourselves,*

*And we shall do it ourselves without any help.*

*How to please God, many times we wonder,*

*Maintaining your workplace neat and clean*

*Is the only answer.*

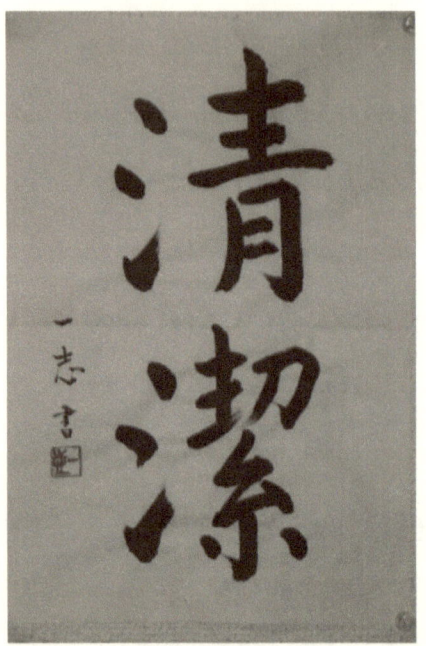

Seiketsu

Calligraphy by Hitoshi Tsuneshige
Japanese Calligrapher

### 8.3.4 Shitsuke

We want to begin with the representation of *shitsuke* using Chinese characters. Shitsuke is written as 躾 in Japanese. 躾 consists of 身 and 美. 身 means human body. The human body has a lot of functional organs and cells. 美 means 'beautiful'. 躾 refers to a beautiful body performing its functions smoothly thanks to the healthy organs, parts and cells doing their job properly. In TPS, the definition of *shitsuke* of 5S is that everybody in the organization adheres strictly to its rules. S*eiri-seiton* was used as a guiding principle for Japanese Samurai families in the past, urging their children to master how to behave, be well-mannered and courteous. There are plenty of rules that they had to follow strictly while behaving naturally, making it look beautiful. According to *shitsuke*, the result is important and failures are not acceptable. A good *shitsuke* means a good result and vice versa. The statement 'I made an effort to educate my child but I couldn't succeed' does not conform to *shitsuke*. A factory in which every employee, including outsourced laborers, follows the rules of the company perfectly would be *shitsuke*. **It would be India's real *shitsuke* when all its nationals stick to the rules and no crime happens in the country. We can not only educate our children in schools but also outside of it, about the importance of observing the rules.** In order to gain a good *shitsuke*, you will need to face hardship and pain. A true and strong India can't be realized if we escape from this hardship and entreat others to appreciate the efforts we put in.

Shitsuke

Calligraphy by Hitoshi Tsuneshige
Japanese Calligrapher

**In Cricket Everyone Follows the Rule**

## 8.4 You Can Learn from Daily Life

It will be interesting to find that TPS is not a sophisticated method but just a faithful execution of the lessons our seniors have been teaching us about life.

### 8.4.1 Go to Bed Early and Get Up Early

Human beings are basically non-nocturnal. Nocturnal animals like bats and owls move at night. The body of a human being is structured to move in the daytime and sleep at night.

Normally, it is not easy to get up early in the morning. A lazy person gets up late in the morning and hurries to office. Many lazy people rush to their office, drive rashly and cause traffic jams. In such situations, they selfishly try to overtake others, almost leading to several traffic accidents.

A lazy person can't work efficiently at office and wastes a lot of time staying longer at office. Such a person is often unable to complete his work before going home. His nocturnal cycle doesn't allow him to sleep. He stays up until midnight. The next morning at office he has to resume his work from the point where he suspended it the previous night. But it is difficult to restart from the exact point where he left his work. This makes him work extra, sometimes beginning things afresh, wasting more time. This is the 'cycle of a devil'.

Although it is not easy to wake up early in the morning, a diligent person makes an effort to get up early. It is easy to commute earlier in the morning. The commuting time is shorter as there are no traffic jams. It is also safer. A commuter who takes the metro can sit on the seat and chalk up a rough plan on the work for the day. He is clear-headed in the morning and he can work effectively, finishing his day's work within the regular time. He never postpones. He knows that his efficiency will be lower if he finishes his job on the way. He goes home before the traffic rush starts and he enjoys his hobbies. As he goes to bed early, it is not hard for him to wake up early the next morning. This is the cycle of an angel. Go to bed early and get up early.

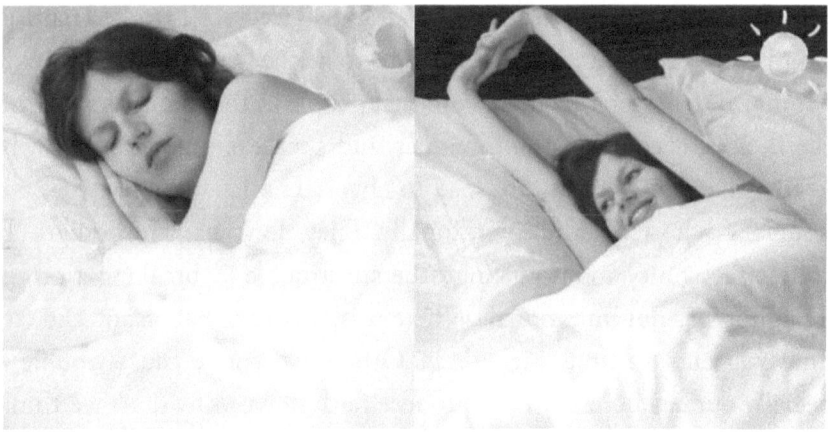

**Early Bird**

## 8.4.2 Don't Tell a Lie!

A child had a quarrel, got defeated and came back crying. His father asked, "What happened?" Judging from his son's explanation, he understood that the opponent was one-sided and irrational. A stupid parent may get mad at the opponent, but a smart parent just does not react. He considers the other side of the story too. He checks the contradictory points. The child might try to justify himself instinctively, making it seem as if he has not committed an offense.

A good parent admonishes his child telling him, "It is not correct to tell untrue things." He is taught that a liar's tongue will be pulled off by the great King Enma. King Enma is prominent in the Japanese culture through Buddhism; he's Yama in Hinduism.

Foreigners are puzzled by Indians' lack of discipline and commitment. They often don't arrive at the scheduled time. They do not deliver within two weeks as promised earlier. A foreigner takes it to be erroneous communication. It is not good for social life as it causes trouble for others. Maybe due to the cultural difference, Indians perceive this problem differently from the Japanese. They promise to come at nine o'clock because they have an intention to do so. This is not a lie at all. "I just wasn't able to come at nine o'clock." They had an intention to report back in two weeks. It is not a lie at all. "I just wasn't able to do it in two weeks." "I worked hard, and I want you to appreciate my effort" seems to be the general way of thinking.

It may be a bit too much to claim that people in India misinform others. Nevertheless, it confuses the foreigner, and such examples are many. It is also true that these confusions lead to chaos. The Japanese feel that a liar is someone who tells a lie intentionally. They don't want to be liars. The Japanese feel guilty about putting others in trouble by breaking a promise although it was not intentional. Whether it is intentional or not, the result is that you end up troubling others. Others whom we cause trouble for, especially our customers, are sure to lose faith in us. Why don't we think it over again?

We have to think again if our people's communication is comprehensible for a foreigner. We may be just sending a wrong message unconsciously. As a result, we may be perceived as untrustworthy.

We must send this information correctly through our traffic systems and organizations. We must keep our appointments. We must meet the specification of our customers and stick to the delivery date. Nobody in the global market will trust those who can't keep promises. No one can succeed in business without trust. We should remember what we used to be told in our childhood: "Don't tell a lie!"

**True and Clear Information**

## 8.4.3 Greet Properly

Good morning! How are you? How do Indians greet? A Westerner smiles at anyone who passes by him in his town. He smiles even at strangers. Asians, including Japanese, hardly smile at strangers. No signals are exchanged. However, when an acquaintance is coming to us, we surely smile at him. Americans smile at anybody they come across in an elevator or on the street. When a Japanese person visited the USA for the first time, he was surprised to see every American smiling at him. As a young girl smiled at him, he misunderstood that she liked him. She was just trying to make him not feel bad.

We should realize the importance of the communication. It is true not only for human relationships in the company but also for the relationship with the customers. If we always send the correct messages, we are likely to receive important messages from others too.

Frankly speaking, a human being is likely to communicate as per his own convenience. Sometimes, his communication emits wrong signals or ones with different meanings, like "no problem". For example, we find vehicles on Indian roads being used wrongly. Horn is not meant for negative communication. Hence it is improper to use it wrongly. In such a case, it is just being used as a weapon. We have to learn more about the importance of communicating information. In Japan or Western countries, almost all drivers use indicators properly before changing lanes, shifting and stopping signals almost immediately.

In India, it is common to find vehicles moving in different directions at the same time. We don't stick to lanes. We use our animal instincts while driving to avoid accidents. We hardly yield to each other, and sometimes, there are unusual fights among people.

A driver may lose his mind when another car suddenly changes direction. He may go crazy if it came toward a different direction instead of the one he indicated. While complaining about the rudeness of other drivers, he himself may not indicate the direction accurately and suddenly change his direction. An egocentric person does not share the right information. Lack of proper communication increase troubles. On the other hand, an altruistic person communicates precisely. More information makes for less trouble. If one of our acquaintances was driving next to us, what would we do? We would be humble enough by communicating well as much as possible and we would yield to him. Why is it impossible to pass the same information to a stranger? Don't you think that needless traffic jams, accidents and hatred are caused by insufficient exchange of information?

Why don't we try saying "after you" to a stranger at the platform of the train station and wait until the passengers get off the train? We used to be told this in childhood: "Greet properly."

Poor communication is one of the factors lowering the productivity of the companies in Japan. There are a lot of enterprises where they are educating managers on the importance of *HouRenSou*, in Japanese language. *HouRenSou* translates to *Houkoku* (report), *Renraku* (inform) and *Soudan* (consult.) Reporting is a subordinate informing his boss on the progress or status of the work assigned to him. This is a duty. A subordinate has to report regularly, irrespective of whether he wants to or not. Informing is simply sharing information with the parties concerned, related to business or work, regardless of the hierarchical relationship at office. Though this is not part of the duty, this is a high-level technique employed by a professional. Can you imagine the kind of information that will make others happy?

Consulting is asking the superior or the colleague for their opinion when it is difficult for you to make a business judgment. Consulting others might be a good idea. Consulting others will foster good interpersonal relationships.

**Greet Properly**

## 8.4.4 Don't Think That Only You Are Right? What a Stupid Boy!

A frog in the well is likely to think that his method of thinking is the best. He feels bad when his way of thinking is derided by others. He feels very uncomfortable. He would deploy a ridiculous logic like "He pointed it out, and it is his fault that I am unhappy!" Take it easy! You are unhappy because you don't have a generous mind. Why don't you try to change your way of thinking totally? This is the awareness revolution. This is supposed to be the most difficult process in any challenge. Human beings are originally conservative. A man believes that his past actions have all been good. The lazier he is, the more likely he is to think this way. So he can't improve himself at all. He can't make *kaizen* in a plant. If you want to improve and promote *kaizen* in your plant, you have to discard your past and seek a new ideal self. Many Indian managers may misunderstand that awareness revolution should be adopted by all employees except themselves. But the awareness revolution should happen at their level first; in other words, it should start from the top management.

This is very difficult. This is the first obstacle to overcome. It is all the more difficult as this is a problem of the mind. When you were a child, don't you remember such kind of conversations? "You think you are best." "No, I don't." "So, follow what I am saying!" "No, it is unpleasant. I do not want to do it."

A child might be gradually mentored by seniors after a long training period. If the spirit of facing challenges is defeated by laziness, one would become a person with narrow views. "The way I understand the best is easy, and the one that I am accustomed to. Therefore, it is the best." However, your performance will hardly go up. "I don't care about the result because I have done it this way until now." But man should advance every day. He has to keep walking until the end of the life. The person who doesn't hope for advancement may return to the life in the primitive age. You can enjoy your life without electricity, car, telephone and so on. There are people who live such a life in extremely remote areas. They never give us any trouble at all. However, men who were born in civilized societies have to work in diligence, improve from the past and better their life from what it is now. In order to do this, a man should change himself every day toward a better direction. This is very hard for a weak or lazy person. Unless you challenge new things with a firm spirit, you can't contribute to your society. Only a courageous spirit can help Indians challenge the global market. A Japanese consultant sometimes recalls that he was often told by his mother in his childhood, "Don't think that only you are right!"

**Frog in the Well**

## 8.4.5 Keep Your Room Clean and Neat!

A man is as a whole sloppy when he is young. Everyone is. This is a story of a Japanese consultant. His room was always dirty and cluttered when he was young, though he liked everything clean and neat. It was troublesome for him to clean up the room and put everything in order. His elder sister visited his room from time to time and often said, "Clean up your room!" When he was out, she cleaned his room for him, saying "There is no other way." His excuse for her complaints was: "It's more comfortable for me this way." Eventually, it was not being cleaned at all. He couldn't find the red pencil. He couldn't find the key. He didn't know where they were. One day, he tried to clean and organize. He found many of the missing stuff. The bottom of the desk was covered by dust and bad odor. It was quite bad for his health as well. One day, a fire almost broke out because of the trash getting burned by cigarette light. It was awfully dangerous. Now he is a consultant who is instructing India to be clean and neat. He sometimes recalls his sister's angry words, "Clean up your room!" with her beautiful eyebrows raised.

Our room, house, garden, company, offices, workplaces at factories, warehouses, public places, roads, inside and outside of the buses, and so on must be kept always clean and neat. We should not keep unnecessary items for a long time thinking they'll be of use some day. We can't use it unless you know where it is, even if it is usable and available. Sort the necessary things out from the unnecessary ones. Put things in order systematically so that you can spot them at a glance. Clean up, without leaving a speck of dust behind. Do it every day. Now that you are doing it, everything is very clean and well organized. You can see at a glance what is there, where and how many. The problem in India is that many factory owners consider 5S as a housekeeping matter. 5S can't be realized unless all members of the company are involved in the factory movement.

Honestly speaking, it is only in the second half of life that an ordinary man can understand the importance of this and its true meaning. Many in India may not understand it now. However, quite a lot of people all over the world have got to understand. India must not fall behind them. We should educate them in their areas, at home and in the company.

**Cleanliness Leads to Higher Efficiency**

## 8.4.6 Brush Your Teeth After a Meal!

I have a toothache today. I have to go to a dentist. Do I have to take a leave today? I can't go to the dentist on Sunday. I can't put up with the pain. It will take more than a week's time to be cured. Do I have to go to the dentist every day to get it cured? What a heavy damage it is! What are you saying? This is because of your sloppy daily life. You are not brushing your teeth properly. The same applies to a car as well. It seldom breaks down with proper maintenance. Don't you find that the equipment in the house you use frequently often breaks down? On an important day, the alarm clock does not work due to lack of battery.

We have to clean everything and every place, just like we have to brush our teeth every day. When we clean something daily, we can spot any abnormality easily. It is the same with the equipment of the factory. Most machine breakdowns are caused by dust and dirt. Frequent cleaning helps us easily find loose bolts before a breakdown occurs. Thus, you can fix any such problem during non-operational periods and you won't need to stop the line for repairs. This is one of the critical duties of an operator. For this, the operator should be well-trained, otherwise, he may not take such things into consideration. We should understand one more thing regarding tooth brushing. If we continue to brush our teeth, we will get into a habit of doing it. At this stage, we can unconsciously implement preventive maintenance, which is called *shitsuke* in TPS.

Top management should recognize it sufficiently. Maintenance is not just repairing a machine when it breaks down, but it is about checking and tuning it to prevent it from breaking down when it's operational. People responsible for maintenance in India's manufacturing industries look awfully busy repairing broken-down machines when the lines stop. We should know the meaning of preventive maintenance. When you were a child, didn't your mother tell you "brush your teeth"?

 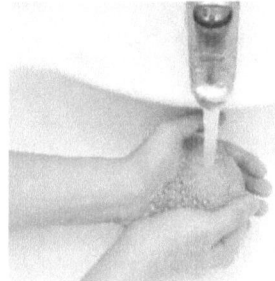

**Brush Your Teeth and Wash Hands**

## 8.4.7 Don't Put Others in Trouble!

A trivial thing has hurt him. Why wasn't I aware of it? It is because of my carelessness. What shall I do? It is still good. He may start reflecting finally. He realizes that what he did was wrong. We sometimes see someone sneaking up a queue as if nothing happened. How will the others waiting patiently in the queue feel? He may think it is none of his business. Someone throws away a lit cigarette butt in the trash. He doesn't feel a sense of guilt. He doesn't even understand that he is putting others at risk. When you are making contact with another person, it should go as perfectly as it does in a baton relay. If you hand over the baton without a warm heart, then there is a high chance that the baton may drop down.

The products or components should be handed over to the customer or to the operator for the next stage of the process after confirming that the quality is perfect. Rejections are unacceptable. This is the original idea of one-piece flow and quality assurance.

Japanese are intently taught this lesson not just during childhood but always. They are educated enough to always know, of how their actions will affect others. A person who comes late to a meeting will have difficulty in succeeding in the Japanese society. "Don't put others in trouble!" is an extremely appropriate reminder in education. India has to stress more on this education. However, a Japanese consultant laments that such education is decreasing in Japan too.

**Examples of Bad Manners**

### 8.4.8 Eat All That You Are Served!

'Eat all that you are served!' is one of important lessons in Japanese education for children. Why waste? Why do you leave out any part of food you are served? Don't be choosy and eat all the food. You should know that vegetables, fish and meat are waiting at the dining table today after someone's great efforts. You should appreciate your food and eat all that you are served.

We should inform in advance if we decide not to eat a particular food. Otherwise, we are ignoring the goodwill of the cook who has made the food for us putting their heart in it. This is a good example of a case where we may put others in trouble. The more privileged we are, the more we have to behave carefully. We have to use all components and materials we make and purchase in the factory. We must not handle anything like leftover food. Why do we create leftovers? Did we purchase too much? Did we produce too much? Did we purchase what we don't consume? We might as well purchase only the necessary items and in sufficient quantity. We will manufacture only the necessary quantity. We can all please our good appetites because we take only what is necessary. We can't cut down on our inventory unless we understand this basic concept. A Japanese consultant said, "Father used to get angry when I left something in my plate."

**Leftover Food Is Being Wasted**

## 8.4.9 Do Your Homework Every Day During Summer Vacation

In Japan, a child is given a lot of homework during the summer holidays. These may include making a picture diary. A child can't help playing during the long holidays.

During the first stage of the holidays, they usually feel that there is enough time. Thus, there is seemingly no problem if he plays with his friends. Soon he finds that time has passed too quickly as he has forgotten to write the diary. I also have homework on handicraft. I have no time to do it. In such a situation, all his family members join in to help complete the homework and his diary is completed. The compulsory homework during summer vacation has a meaning. Some opine it's better to let children play as much as they like during summer vacation. However, this kind of training is for the children to acquire the power of independence in future. They will learn how to allot time for the duties they have to perform. To maintain a diary, perseverance is required and the tenacity of spirit can be raised through such work or effort. What is most important is that you train your mind to reflect and challenge to prepare a better plan next time. Children easily learn or realize that they can do a big or seemingly impossible thing if they do a small part every day. They learn that they can't get a good result through patchwork because it is likely to be accompanied by mistakes, rejections or dead stock. This relates to the concept of leveled production. Continuing uniform and sustained operation leads you to action, maintenance and education with ease. Homework during summer vacation makes most children feel miserable. But just a few children are likely to succeed like excellent companies.

**A Boy at a Loss with Homework**

### 8.4.10 Do Not Join in Your Child's Quarrel!

Parents often say they are not children to be sermonized to. In Japan, this is a proverb. Your child comes back crying after a quarrel with another kid. You ask, "What happened?" Your child presents his one-sided view against his opponent. "It is inexcusable!" you say. You go to the opponent to scold them. He can't tell you anything out of fear. He goes home and tells the story to his father. His father too gets upset and it blows up into a big quarrel between adults of two families. This was a quarrel between kids. Either of you can't take full responsibility, even though the matter is trivial. If parents go on with this kind of behavior, the child becomes habituated to seek the parent's power even for trivial things. He becomes a kid who doesn't make an effort. He is always incomplete. Therefore someone has to make up for his insufficiency. He can never become full-fledged or complete. Similarly, when you have excess inventory to protect against the machine breakdown, quality problem and material shortage, you will rely on them endlessly. As you have enough on the inventory, you can't find problems and solve them. You don't have the ability to do it either. The situation is similar to that of a child who can't become strong due to his parent's frequent interventions.

These things have been taught from childhood by parents and seniors. Many humans can't fully make use of these valuable lessons. In Toyota and other excellent companies across the globe, all employees observe what they have to do as responsible human beings considering it a part of the total culture of the company.

A lazy man misinterprets that a diligent man has a magic wand. The lazy man thinks that anyone can use the magic wand and tries to learn only how to use it. However, he is unable use this magic wand and gets upset thinking it is defective. He doesn't know that he has to transform into a diligent man first to use the magic wand effectively. A lazy man usually doesn't realize that he is lazy. An actually diligent man worries every day that he is being lazy. Don't you think this is also one of the greatest lessons?

**Intervention in a Child's Fight**

## 8.5 Lean and Waste

### 8.5.1 What Does 'Lean' Mean?

According to the Oxford dictionary, 'lean' means efficient and involving no waste, in an industry or company. It means thin, especially healthily so, without any superfluous fat in a person or animal. It means 'containing little fat of meat'. But it also has a negative meaning: an unrewarding substance or nourishment. Let us conclude here that lean manufacturing or lean management refers to high efficiency and little waste.

**'Lean' Means Efficient. The Wrestler Is as Efficient as the Athlete.**

### 8.5.2 Efficiency

What are the factors that reduce the efficiency of a company? Indirect segments like support services, management and marketing should identify seven wasteful ways besides driving manufacturing. It is true, not only in India but also around the world, that there are insufficient efforts to reduce waste in indirect segments. Everything is related to costs. We should know by now that lesser expense and higher income are quite possible.

In case of wastes in production, it is easier for us to understand if we think of operational availability. Let us explain operational availability in short, for ease of understanding. The production line should not be operated

24 hours a day. There are several things that need to be done for keeping or maintaining the line in proper capability or shape. Morning meeting, change-over, transfer of duty, 5S of machine and workplace, preventive maintenance of machines and education should all be done taking some time off operation.

The time left after the above activities can be used or considered for operation. A target operational time should be determined taking wastage into account. The line may stop due to a machine breakdown, set-up or material shortage, and it will make rejections. We have to make drastic efforts to reduce these wastes. In order to do this, we may at times need a project team and follow-up by top management.

We have to always consider the efficiency of indirect and marketing divisions. It is difficult to keep a tab as it's impossible to exercise control visually. We can see in some cases that improper exchange of information between these divisions and production creates plenty of wastes, but only the production division usually suffers. Information from marketing and customers changes often and widely. Production and delivery divisions have to correspond to or meet such volatility by maintaining huge inventories. This undermines the strength of a company, like what malignant cholesterol does to the human body.

We will always need to have the correct and updated information from customers and your dealers. The information from the customer is the starting point of the river stream. Wrong and improperly timed exchange of information will certainly cause chaos in the downstream. Top management must rectify this.

Products handled by a dealer or shop could be fluctuated and the undulation easily handled depending on the total area. But actually, many of India's factories are suffering from sudden and big production change. This is caused by inappropriate control of information due to the laziness of the upstream management of the company. In the Toyota system, stable productions in factories and minimum inventories are required in order to minimize the lead time required to deliver products to customers.

We have to look at things through the prism of defective waste in indirect divisions. We must not consider these divisions as privileged ones.

We often do insufficient documentation and repair work. We conduct or attend a lot of meetings that do not start on schedule and never conclude. We make others work with wrong information. These are all wasteful because of a defect.

There are other kinds of wastes in indirect division. They say that more than 90 percent of the indirect work in an average company in the world is wasteful. Aren't the figures much higher in India? Another problem regarding this matter is that the top management and indirect staff consider themselves privileged and don't feel the need to make an effort to reduce waste in their work.

Efforts on efficiency increase can be truly meaningful only if we address the indirect division as well as production division. Before we drive any such reforms, we must learn what waste is and what is meaningful to your company's life. As we mentioned before, Japan has already started reducing indirect wastes through the *Hou-Ren-Sou* concept.

### 8.5.3 All Costs Come from Personnel and Labor

In general understanding, cost includes material, labor, depreciation, overhead and other expenses. But you should realize that cost only includes spend on personnel and labor. The cost of the materials we buy is the personnel and labor cost incurred by the material maker. Depreciation of machines is covered by their cost. The cost of machines comes from the personnel and labor cost of its makers. Now we understand that lean management means 'management of human ability'. Human beings possess excellent abilities. Yet at times, they can't perform to their potential. TPS will help us learn how to draw out the human abilities.

### 8.6 Seven Wastes of TPS

The automobile industry in the United States in the 1920s reduced cost greatly and wooed the middle-class customers. Middle-class citizens, who had not been able to afford a vehicle earlier, could purchase a car, due to affordable pricing. Not only the automotive industry but the consumer electric industry too reduced costs by going for mass production. A flow assembly line was developed and the new age was ushered in. A lot of families started enjoying the use of washing machines and refrigerators in their homes. In India, washing machines, refrigerators and color TV may have been the three sacred treasures of the upper-middle class. In the United States, at the same time, the three sacred treasures of the middle class were: passenger cars, washing machines and refrigerators. As a matter of fact, in current India, washing machines, refrigerators, color TVs and automobiles are driving the growth of the economy. Communication devices are also contributing greatly. The United States reduced cost through mass production and met the expectation of the middle class.

Viewing this from the consumer side, there were a few limitations. Everyone had the same or similar models due to fewer types or varieties being made available. It is usual for individual consumers to have different tastes. Toyota directed its attention to this aspect. Mass produced, low-priced products could satisfy the expectations of consumers to some degree, but consumers were gradually getting tired and monotonous due to the lack of options. Toyota then set out to manufacture products that satisfied individual consumers. For this, they needed to be able to produce a variety of products in smaller quantities. But the costs would be high as the quantity in each batch is lesser. They thought of ways to counter the situation. They discovered that all manufactures produced wastes. Not everything can be converted into a different form. The advanced gasoline internal combustion engine effectively used up only around 50 percent of the usual energy required. A lot of energy was wasted through heat emissions. In due course, the waste was reduced through new technologies like hybrid.

What we can do is reduce the waste as much as possible. The energy efficiency of the company can be equated to the minimum possible expense invested toward customer satisfaction divided by the total expense incurred. The total waste can be measured calculating the difference between total expense and the minimum expense required for customer satisfaction. The customer never pays for wasted portions. Toyota identified the wastes and classified them into seven categories. Toyota Production System focused on methods and efforts to reduce wastes.

An absolute condition is that the system (not just the TPS) must work. For this, every member of the organization has to follow the rules faithfully and obediently. It may seem to be very impractical in a company with a culture of breaking rules easily. Awareness revolution and respect for systems is the only way to success.

In India's foreign-based companies, including Japan-based ones, non-Indian employees are coaching tenaciously, trying to demonstrate and promote efficient production systems. But such companies are worried about the cost of non-Indian employees. There are fewer foreign-based companies in India compared to other countries. If we rely only on leadership from foreign countries, we may have Indian quality products produced at the same costs as developed countries. Unless we, as true patriotic Indians, kick-start an awareness revolution in the manufacturing industry (there are a few common aspects in agriculture too) and promote a culture of minimizing waste as much as possible, we can't genuinely help build India's economic power.

Before we begin, we need to recognize an important thing. Waste depends upon the purpose and the definition of waste is not absolute. The following seven categories of wastes should be applied only in TPS. There are no wastes when we have no purposes.

### 8.6.1 Overproduction

"You have made a lot of food! How many guests do you have today?" "Five guests will come." "It might be a bit too much, isn't it?" "It would be better than dissatisfying them with less food." The guests may actually appear to have enjoyed dinner. In China, it is considered to be good entertainment to provide food more than the guest can eat. As a matter of fact, due to too many options and the ample amount; a guest eats only a little bit of every dish, leaving the rest. The remaining food is discarded as leftovers. Of course, it is costly. When you receive hospitality in China on almost every occasion, we feel sorry about the leftovers. On the other hand, we appreciate the hospitality. Now let us compare the situation with our manufacturing industries. According to a Japanese consultant, the production management of most of the Indian manufacturing companies look uncertain and exercise insufficient control over plans and actual implementation. Production may vary and could be in short supply or in excess.

In a global excellence company, overproduction almost never happens. In India, overproduction occurs frequently. This is caused by inefficient management of the actual working place. Overproduction is to produce more than the planned amount. When will we stick to the plan? Operators had enough time and materials, perhaps more than the required amount planned earlier. The number and quantity during batch operations in the medium process can't be controlled. In the worst-case scenario, operation is suspended halfway. From the point of view of production management, overproduction may lead to the creation of dead stock. In such companies, they constantly have machine, material, quality and labor problems during the operating periods. Depending on the level of operational troubles or cycle time, sometimes operators can finish earlier than scheduled. Some operators then disappear from the workplace while others still continue the operation. A Japanese consultant suspects that they expect to be praised. Production plan should be made taking the maximum capacity of operators into account. Short production cycles should be adjusted by overtime operation. Early finishing time should be adjusted and employed for the improvement of cycle time. The extra time should be used for cleaning and maintenance of the machine and so on. In India, the relationship between production line and materials and components seems to be not so smoothly linked with each other, and most factories end up working too much in the process. Inventory is called a devil in Japan, but many think of it as an angel that hides problems. Production plan should be made based on actual sales trend to minimize inventories.

Production is meaningless without matching the plan. We should understand that we must not produce more than the proposed amount. It should be controlled by a strict rule. As for the violation, it should be taken as a serious foul act. The shoulder of the road is always kept open for ambulance and fire engine, no matter how congested the traffic gets in Japan, Europe and America. Almost all drivers observe this rule. In India, the ambulance can't move forward during congestion. This is because drivers in India don't observe the rules. This is comparable to the scene in a factory.

Overproduction is a violation of PDCA. We can change the plan after checking. We should know that the operation needs an everyday rhythm, but overproduction spoils the rhythm.

**Overproduction is the Violation of the Rule**

## 8.6.2 Inventory

Whenever a Japanese consultant visits an Indian factory, he finds it full of inventory with some exceptions. According to his assessment, it is almost impossible to determine what, where and how many. He often asks, "How many of this part number do you have right here?" But there is no answer. "You are not taking control." He tries to convey this message to the person-in-charge. The person-in-charge often feels annoyed at his observation and reacts thus, "I am controlling. The data is being controlled by computer."

If he requests to see the data, it reaches him over 30 minutes later. "Do the actual figures match the computer data?" "…"

First of all, messiness makes it impossible to count the real figure. According to the computer, they have enough of a particular part and should not make fresh purchases. But they can't find this part number in the mess and this situation may bring about a line stop because of material shortage. Despite its availability, they can't access or use it. So they purchase the part again, incurring an additional expense. Inventory occupies space. Space translates to cost. This is another kind of waste. This waste sometimes causes further waste in the form of transportation. Toyota dislikes excess inventory and overproduction. TPS explains that inventory is a devil. Inventory is not only wasteful but also harmful. Inventory spoils hard-working persons, including business runners and managers. Business is a competition. You should always be improving your mind by working hard. High inventory can cause adverse changes like making the people in the company lazy.

For example, we don't address our quality, material, machine problems and absenteeism because we have enough inventories. Unless we have sufficient inventories, we face the serious problem of line stops. We may put our customer in trouble. But if we always strive to make sure that we do not put others in trouble, we will not allow troubles concerning equipment, material, quality and labor. In order to minimize all the troubles, we have to work hard as professionals.

**A Big Inventory Is Also a Devil**

## 8.6.3 Processing

"There are many policemen in India. Why so?" "There are many wrongdoers and we need plenty of policemen to clamp down on them." "They are controlling traffic at intersections without traffic lights." "Yes, they do it sometimes at junctions with traffic lights too. Policemen have to work at intersections where there is heavy traffic but no lights, but if everyone sticks to rules, you don't need so many policemen." We need policemen to watch people who may not abide by rules. Too many people breaking the rules is a problem, isn't it? India's system is often so complicated, don't you think so? Is it impossible to simplify it? Someone said to me, "A simple system makes corruption difficult." Corruption occurs when a man with a weak mind finds power and falls prey to temptation like others. It is very difficult to eliminate corruption because it includes people who are into illegal gain to meet their living expenses.

In a factory, they oversee the machine, material, assemble components and inspect products. But all the processes are surprisingly regarded as wastes in TPS, baffling us. The customer only pays for the finished goods. Therefore, we have to make an effort to minimize the wastes by developing new methods of mechanizing, assembling and reducing inspection by improving quality levels. Unless we think of it as a waste, we will not make an effort to reduce it. In fact, any effort or process that does not add value to the customer is a waste, as the customer is not paying for it.

In the manufacturing industry, all processes produce wastes and minimizing the waste is the key to efficiency improvement. It is nonsensical to double and triple the inspection process in order to deliver perfect products because we evidently have no confidence in the process or trust workers as professionals. We should think of inspection as a waste. Ideally, we should be able to make anything without inspection. Quality is built during the process of manufacturing. Any amount of inspection is simply a post-mortem.

**Processing**

## 8.6.4 Motion

There is a common thing in martial arts. Examples of martial arts are boxing, fencing, wrestling, kendo, judo and so on. The common thing in martial arts is that the stronger fighter moves lesser. The weaker fighter moves unnecessarily and tires out, giving a chance for his opponent to attack. He never wins. 頓 *(-ton)* of 整理整頓 *(seiri-seiton)* means 'to be steady and static'. In case of human beings, it means maintaining perfect composure. What about a restless person? Can someone who is always shaking his body or jiggling his knees come across as convincing to others? Even though he is speaking the right thing, he might not be believed or taken seriously due to his nervousness. We should not move wastefully. We should study the wasteful movements of each operator in the factory. We can reduce wasteful movement of hands and body by improving the layout of the material supply unit. Materials that need to be assembled should be kept within the arm's length. This kind of *kaizen* can be achieved by an improvement in the design of the working table, including material bins. Is this matter too trivial to be studied seriously? We should exhibit sufficient sense as professionals working under the *kaizen* culture. We are often saying *kaizen, kaizen*. But we should actually make *kaizen*, not just speak about it. Global excellence companies are fighting desperately to improvise on such small points day by day.

**Motion**

## 8.6.5 Transportation

Only logistics service providers find it useful to carry things. Airline services and transportation industries make money by carrying humans or goods. But when we provide customers with our products and our services, they have no idea about who moves what in our company. Our customer will be satisfied if he receives the specified product he requested for and by the taste of the cuisine and warm-hearted services we provide. Our customer is not interested in the number of times your staff makes a business trip. What satisfies the customer is the quality of products and services in terms of meeting the specifications and requirements.

It is wasteful to move men and goods. You have to minimize this. When you make a layout of workshops and offices, a sporadic layout in a large space automatically leads to movement of humans and goods. You need to have a basic idea to minimize movements, like opting for a compact layout, linear movement and lesser business trips and so on.

We often go wrong in investing too much in the beginning. We may think that a big initial investment in business would make it more efficient. Nice automatic long conveyers look so modern and highly industrialized. An automatic warehouse is cool and efficient. First of all, it is not good to spend unnecessarily. We should realize that the transportation of goods, men and storage of goods is wasteful and affects availability of spaces and machines.

**Transportation**

## 8.6.6 Waiting

"Do I have to change trains at this station? I have to wait 3 hours. It will take 10 hours to reach the destination, even though the train travel time is only 7 hours." Anybody can understand that 3 hours are being wasted here. Do meetings or discussion sessions start at the scheduled time here in India? How many are coming on time? Can you blame officers or persons with higher statures usually coming late? A lot of people earning high salaries are just waiting, doing nothing. Too much money is being paid to those who are doing nothing. While talking to someone, his mobile phone rings. He picks up. He tells us, "One minute," but his conversation over the phone never stops. We cannot do anything while waiting. This is awfully wasteful. In a factory, during line stops due to machine trouble or material shortage, operators have to wait until the line recovers. Sometimes, operators in factories disappear before we know. After returning, they explain that they had gone to get water and taken a long time due to the distance to the availability point. We often come across similar situations in case of a line operator, who may be found talking over the mobile phone while others are waiting. Don't you think all these are wasteful?

The problem is that most people do not consider them to be wasteful. They feel that it's okay because it's a minor thing. Top management folks who come late to the meeting are not qualified to blame others for being late. We should recognize that the sloppy attitude of the top management makes operators shoddy. We have to minimize the meeting period. In order to do that, everybody has to come on time. Documents should be prepared nicely in advance. We should explain efficiently. In Japan, there are some companies where meetings are held while standing. We should think of the mobile phone as a devil. We should finish mobile conversations within one minute. It generates more waste. Operators are not allowed to leave the line except during the break times. Operators can seek permission from supervisor if there is an emergency. Machines must not break down and material shortage must not happen during an operation. The person-in-charge has to take responsibility if the line stops due to any reason.

**Waiting**

### 8.6.7 Rejection

Even a child understands that rejection is bad and wasteful. Rejection is a mistake. The following is the scene that can be seen often here. There are plenty of unfinished goods lying along the assembling line. "What are these?" "These are rejections. No problem. These are repairable, I will do it later." Another bunch is found in a hidden place. "What are these?" "These are rejections. These are not repairable." The irreparable ones are kept hidden. The mentality is that they are hiding them because they don't want them to be seen. The repairable ones can be returned to the line, but the irreparable ones can't be and these are kept hidden to avoid bothering about them. This is caused by lack of standards at work. The hiding place of irreparable goods becomes the grave of rejects. Such operations don't help quality analysis and improvement. Making rejects, using material for making rejects and repairing rejections are all wastages.

Any rejection has causes. No rejection will happen if you can eliminate all causes. In such a company as mentioned above, rejections are never reduced. In fact, rejections occur more and more due to lack of analysis and inaction. Unless we strongly believe that we will never allow rejections to flow out, they will never end. It is a simple story: if everyone in the company was a real professional and his work always perfect, how could we make any rejects?

In an average factory, everybody seems amateur and always thinks that all responsibility rests on others. The virus of rejection thrives in such places.

**Rejection**

## 8.7 Mainstream

The purpose of TPS is to minimize wastes in the enterprise. There is an order to taking action. However, it will not succeed unless we follow this order. We must not disregard this order. We also know a manager with insufficient deliberation is likely to pay attention to only popular things like *poka-yoke* and *kanban*. This is one of the causes that makes it difficult to succeed. There is a rule in advance TPS. We should consider the importance of the rule and it is not to be disregarded. It is not to say that the rule cannot be changed. We should get into the habit of changing the rule by following PDCA. Studying the stream of TPS is meaningful. The main slogan of Toyota Production System is awareness revolution, 5S, flow production, standardized work and leveled production. This stream should be supported by exercising visual control and employing flexible manpower. Let us go over this one by one.

### 8.7.1 Awareness Revolution

As we mentioned before, most business runners of excellent companies are well aware of the importance and difficulties associated with awareness revolution. This is the starting point. When we decide to do something, we need to make a strong resolution. A weak resolve can't overcome the hardships or adversities we have to face before reaching the destination or we won't reach the destination after all. A weak or lazy man tries to make the most effort to find excuses for not doing something.

Awareness revolution doesn't work without follow-up action. It is like our chant to our God every morning. When we recite our daily duties in front of God, our resolve becomes firmer.

In a Japanese department store, every clerk shouts, "Good morning! Thank you very much! Please come again!" every morning before the opening of the store. Repeating the everyday shouts improves their resolve to take good care of customers.

In some of the excellent companies and factories, the staff members shout their resolutions and recite what they have to do each morning. Without the leadership of top managers, subordinates will never follow. Lean manufacturing is implemented by managers. Let us see some examples. These poems are being used in some Japanese companies and a Japanese consultant has translated them:

*Change Corus*

*You! Weak person! Roger!*

*Change, change, change your workplace!*

**Make your workplace change, and you can change yourself!**

*Make change, change your workplace!*

*Make change, change, radical change! Roger!*

*Change Chorus*

*You! Strong person! Roger!*

*Change, change, change yourself!*

**Change yourself, and you can change your workplace!**

*Change, change, change yourself!*

*Make change, change, radical change! Roger!*

**A Strong Resolution**

## 8.7.2  5S

The original Japanese meanings of 5S were mentioned in 8.3. 5S is the basis of everything. All companies, stores and restaurants, including those in Japan, that think little of 5S are all unexceptionally less competitive. In the Toyota Production System, 5S is regarded as the most important point, as a basis for efficiency and quality, and all members of the organization are expected to understand its importance.

Negligence of 5S may not affect anything immediately but will result in lazy people getting tired of it. In some countries, 5S implementation is considered to be a housekeeper's job. We should recognize that every country or factory of excellence everywhere is clean. It is regretful that some business managers are making little use of 5S. They only have a theoretical knowledge of it.

*Seiri* (sort out) is defined as segregating the necessary and the unnecessary. In this case, we should have a clear idea of what is necessary and unnecessary. We act upon it through *seiton*. We should check on it through *seisou*. We go back to the amendment of the original plan and review using *seiketsu*. 4S is like PDCA. 5S, as we mentioned already, is the ideal style of functioning in the organization where everybody strictly follows the rules of the company.

### 8.7.3 Flow Production (One Piece Flow)

When the economy is growing rapidly, mass production of batches is effective in cost reduction, ensuring a higher speed and a shorter cycle time. However, we have to be very cautious about quality control when there is batch production. There is a high risk or possibility that quality or inventory problems may occur during mass production. Currently, India practices batch or mass production style, even though most of the managers in India may not agree.

When a manager explains the process of operating a flow production in a manufacturing company in India, we come across a lot of cases of batch style operations. Operators think that lot operation, in which plenty of components are placed on the working table, can be assembled quickly while assembling one after the other is troublesome. They take the process apart and repeat the same action, instead of following the whole process.

The speed of assembling in a batch may be quicker for one piece. However, the priorities of the operators seem to be to finish quickly rather than to make products carefully. This may bring about quality problems and overproduction due to lack of concentration and attentiveness and a lack of sense of mission to produce a good product.

Usually, when operators go on a break, they leave several items that are still under production on the table. In this case, it is very difficult to control quantity and quality. They leave unfinished items, which can't be shown in drawings, on the table, increasing the possibility of slip-ups or big mistakes.

A zero-defect goal is unattainable unless our operators are professional. A professional technique can't be transferred to the products unless each process is completed one by one as regulated. A professional operator should assemble the components and parts conforming to the quality standards for each component and part. The operator should not deliver defects for the next process, as the next level operator is his real customer.

We have many operators who have insufficient awareness as professionals in India's manufacturing industries due to lack of or inadequate education. For them, value lies in not providing excellent products to customers but in earning more money for lesser work. The result of this way of thinking becomes visible natural in workplaces. As they want to escape the perils of hard work, they take the quickest route and the simplest work. This is why a batch of rejects even occurs in a flow line.

An individual in a factory or a company must prioritize his customers. An excellent artist concentrates on each process and works carefully from the heart to work without failure. We can't make a good product, even with a high-level machine, without sincerity. This is where the importance of the concept of one-piece flow production is. The top management in manufacturing industries in the country have to first educate their workers so that they think on those lines. This is the responsibility of the management. A professional never makes any defects, but non-professional inspectors will not stop defects from flowing out.

**A Professional Artist's Work**

## 8.7.4 Standard Work

There is logic in the form and practice of golf or cricket and it is difficult to improve quickly if it is not followed. We can all improve in our own ways to a certain degree. We can improve technically and faster with the help of a professional coach. This is the importance of education.

How does it work? If we pay our coach, we are expected to listen to him seriously. We often don't listen to our parents and teachers in school, though our parents are paying the fees. This is typical of a child and it is a senseless attitude for a professional to have.

The basic purpose of having a standard at work is to follow it obediently as determined by rules. In sports, we are to be disqualified for violating the rule. But the average Indian driving on the road breaks rules without any hesitation. It is evident from the traffic situation in India. Highly educated as well as ordinary drivers violate the rules. Such drivers may just think "If I am okay, it's okay." A material handler in India harbors the same attitude. He may like to supply in big batches so that he will have more free time for enjoyment or relaxing.

Standards should be developed after thorough study. Nobody would follow instructions made irresponsibly by a lazy teacher. He (the teacher or the supervisor) must study what waste is and how to reduce it, intensively, and develop a meaningful standard. In a manufacturing factory, tact time is decided by the production plan, manpower layout, standard operation of each process, and machine maintenance; the 5S of machine and workplace are decided accordingly. All team members then operate as decided in the work standard.

In India, we find nice work standards in the cabin crews' safety demonstration in airplanes. Many dancers in Bollywood can move synchronously and excellently with the music. These are typical examples of high work standards. We can't create one immediately until we graduate, undergoing some severe training.

In India's average manufacturing industries, it is quite usual to find that work standards are only vague explanations. There is no mention of vital details, no efforts to impart training and no follow-ups on adherence. But it's obviously possible to have such standards as you find good examples in airlines and Bollywood. We must create a situation where everybody follows rules as regulated.

**Bollywood Dancers Do Not Violate Rules in Their Performance**

## 8.7.5 Leveled Production

The best situation, as everyone understands, is when we manufacture the same products and quantities daily. But surprisingly, there are a lot of changes made in the production plan in Indian manufacturing factories. Some Indian manufacturing companies apply the *kanban* system. They may not understand the true meaning of *kanban* system but top managements invariably prefer to use the term.

Except foreign car manufacturers, almost all Indian manufacturing companies can't explain how they make the *kanban* system work in a leveled production set-up. For example, if we could make daily production plan with a 10 percent variation, then we would be able to distribute manpower properly and prepare parts easily minimizing inventories.

But how does an actual situation look like? Sometimes a huge number of parts without *kanban* can be found around the *kanban* post. You may proudly proclaim to be following the Toyota Production System, which you admire. It is very common to note a big fluctuation in the production plan disturbing the production site, as they operate neglecting the *kanban* system. Indirect support and service divisions may be without sufficient knowledge about *kanban*.

The Indian industry, as a whole, seems to be not making the effort to gain and control the information upstream. Incorrect information and abrupt change in production plans may baffle the downstream completely.

We must understand that even though actual sales results of an individual dealer may be highly fluctuating, the situation of the total market (i.e. all dealers' results) must be undulated and stable. If you control this undulation, you may eventually be able to make a stable daily production plan in a week. This kind of leveled production will help us utilize *kanban* well and easily for frequent material feeding to minimize inventory. In order to do this, rather than just focusing on factory, marketing division needs to put in more effort and exercise higher level production control.

There is another thing that we should understand. Leveled production is a high-level process, but it can be operated easily. A skier employing a good technique will be able to choose a safer route on the slope. An excellent golfer can hit a ball further without extra power. They will be able to do that after training long and hard.

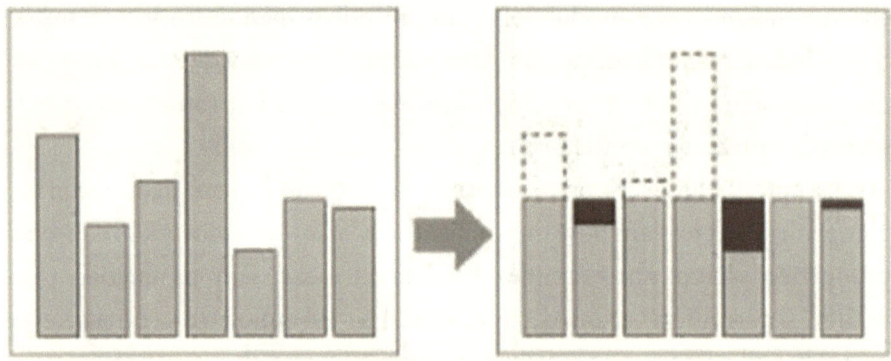

**Levelled Production**

## 8.8 Visual Control

Visual control is a way of management that helps to find out problems about material, equipment and quality, easily. The flow is from quality assurance, preventive maintenance, and to *kanban*. The essence of TPS is to find the problem at once and take action immediately. As we mentioned before, we must remember the best person to learn visual control from is a blind person. He can do anything even in the dark because he keeps everything arranged. He can visualize everything through his mind's eyes. This is real visual control.

### 8.8.1 Quality Assurance

From the consultant's experience, there still seems to be many Indian managers who misunderstand that quality assurance is the same as inspection. The basic point is satisfying the customers by keeping the promise made to them. The promise is usually made after an approval of the drawing or by specification. In order to manufacture, a supplier showcases his internal drawings or a list of options and produces according to it. Workers also must be aware of the internal promise. We should also recognize that no rejection would occur if it is produced as per the drawings, as they are considered perfect documents like scriptures, which should not be violated.

However, a human being is imperfect and makes mistakes. Fewer mistakes create fewer rejects and higher quality. There are some statistical methods to decide on the safety zone from the variations in quality assurance. But we need to consider one more thing in India. This is the fact that many people break rules without any hesitation. We must recognize that there are a lot of workers who employ batch operation processes for their conveniences, in spite of the regulation being in place for a one-piece flow line. If every worker clearly understands what he has to do, as part of the process, including the inspection, he must do it before passing it over to the next process; then rejections would hardly happen.

Quality assurance is not aimed at segregating defect through inspection; its objective is to avoid making any defects in the manufacturing process. A worker who thinks of the next process head as his customer will never make any defective piece. This sense of the worker is similar to the feeling of a mother toward her small child. She is always anxious about her son or daughter. She will worry that he or she may stumble, be bitten by an animal, eat strange things or get others in trouble. She always thinks negatively. It is the mother's love to take measures to avoid unexpected things from happening. If we had such kind of love for our customers, we would never produce any defects. The defect is an evidence of inadequate thought being put into our customers.

Don't you think there are a lot of rejections hidden in the factories of this country? This is not allowed in TPS. Rejections and defects are to be controlled visually and measures taken immediately. A human being is likely to wish to hide things that are inconvenient for him to face. This kind of feeling impedes progress. In TPS, all rejections are displayed so that everyone can see them and act upon them during the day. If we hide, we forget to take action. This is like exposing a rule breaker in public. In Toyota, all problems are used as improvement opportunities. With such continuous improvement happening, customers are generally delighted.

### 8.8.2 Preventive Maintenance

First of all, we should understand the difference between repair and maintenance. We are traveling by car and say it breaks down. What could be usually expected in such a situation?

The glitch creates a traffic jam. We have to call for a repair service. We cannot reach our potential customer's place and we fail to procure a new business. We can spot a broken-down vehicle every ten minutes in Delhi. Broken-down vehicles are usually not parked at the side of the road unlike in Japan or other advanced countries. They may be found imposingly in the center of the road. An average Japanese person will predict when a glitch is likely to occur in his vehicle. He will pull his vehicle to the side before it goes out of control. In his mind, he doesn't want to hinder others' work due to his problem. We need to cultivate this attitude.

We should always check our car or company vehicles to avoid bothering others. This is the key point about maintenance. The operation manual guides us on when and what we have to do, and it may have been explained while buying the vehicle. However, we do not follow such regulations because it's troublesome or it may cost us. Often, this is why our car stops suddenly while traveling. It's too inconvenient. This is because we are not considerate enough toward others.

Unlike repair, maintenance demands considerably high engineering and management methods. We can't perform this without deep study. Lazy people will not be able to do it. Maintenance is similar to medical science. A huge amount of data is collected and classified, and the characteristics of diseases found, a cure developed and implemented. In the case of contagious diseases, even the details like the route of transmission of the infection are investigated.

We should collect huge amounts of data like this about machines, devices, consumable parts, characteristics of suppliers and lead time of spare parts, and make plans, formulate rules and regulations on preventive maintenance and abide by it. When we stick to the rules, we may seldom find breakdown of machines and can try to improve. These data and maintenance plans are controlled visually. If we keep data and plans only on the computer, we can't keep our machines and equipment in a healthy and proper condition. If we control visually, the maintenance will surely work. Maintenance should be respected and repair should be disdained.

### 8.8.3 Kanban

We can easily understand that *kanban* is a tool for visual control. *Kanban* can visually control our components and products and regulate quantities and determine locations.

Many companies, including Japanese ones, are eager to introduce the *kanban* system. India is not an exception either. Without *kanban*, there is no Toyota Production System. We must recognize that *kanban* is considerably difficult to implement without mastering the fundamental steps. It is just like challenging a sound sports technique without training, or without a stronger foundation or limbs in your body.

We must also recognize that the *kanban* system is a team sport, unlike figure skating in which an individual performs alone. Federal and local government management are also sports teams. In team sports, everybody has to keep to the rules and proceed toward a common destination. Is it possible in current India to stick to the *kanban* system?

Several Indian factories put up *kanban* posts, without any evidence of them using the *kanban* system. The word '*kanban*' can be found displayed. But it is difficult to determine how they are operating. They might have just wanted to display the term '*kanban*'.

What is the purpose for which they are using *kanban*? Is only the term important for them? As they are not well-trained in their lower body, it doesn't yield results. We have to begin by getting every member in the company to strictly observe the rules. Before that, we must understand the *kanban* rules just like we have to conform to the specifications our customer is requesting.

*Kanban* works well in the leveled production situation. But in the big fluctuating production situation, *kanban* may become a simple pull system and create extra inventories even though it is meant for minimizing them. *Kanban* doesn't work if we carry defects along. Needless to mention, *kanban* system can't work if 5S is not in place. Let us try to learn more about the two-bin system.

The concept of the two-bin system is easy to understand. In the actual manufacturing site in India, they are hardly using this method correctly. This system is for avoiding material shortage using minimum inventories. As a whole, workers and material handlers are not operating as per the rule due to inadequate awareness or the insufficient understanding of the management. Even supervisors are not aware of it and are thus unable to give any advice.

In the two-bin system, we must arrange the parts in two bins of holding quantities. And each bin will contain the quantity shown in the bin. A worker has to use parts from only one designated bin. When this bin becomes empty, he must place this empty bin in the return chute and continue work, picking up parts from the other bin. Meanwhile, the material handler must resupply the designated quantity of the required part. This is one kind of *kanban* system. The bin has all the necessary information on it. The *kanban*, in this case, is the bin itself containing the information.

Even the use of stationery items can be controlled by a similar system of two bin system. If we put a note on one saying "please purchase" before the last one is empty, you can avoid material shortage.

In India's manufacturing industries, we think we should take a note of the insufficient education among workers and supervisors. The worst case is that top management shoots its mouths without understanding the essence. Thus, the top management doesn't demonstrate to their workers and staff. This is a bad condition prevailing in the manufacturing industries.

In India, we think a lot of industries are using the two-bin system. They are using two boxes for the same parts. The two boxes are almost always full and overflowing with parts with no mention about quantity. Even if a quantity is mentioned, the level of accuracy is dubious. There is no trace of the boxes having ever moved. The material handler is supplying parts to both the boxes and the workers using them. One box would have been much better.

The above case clearly shows that they are only using only the terminology for the two-bin system, without understanding the meaning or sense of it. There may be many examples like this in this country. When the top management wants to start something, they must thoroughly understand the purpose and the meaning of it first. *Kanban* is like a relay baton. It has information, command and value. *Kanban* would become meaningless with wrong information sharing and handling. A wrong usage of *kanban* will necessitate more inventories.

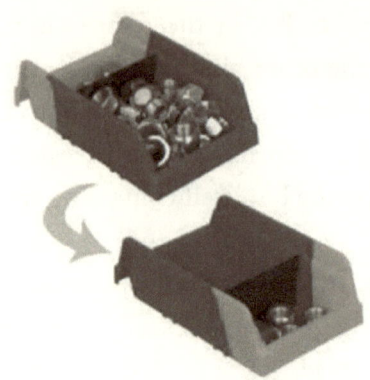 

**Two Bins and Baton of Relay**

## 8.9 Flexible Manpower

Another sub-flow of TPS is flexible manpower. This is to produce any quantity of anything anytime, with a low cost. We must be able to produce with any number of operators available. A production line needing more than a definite number of operators doesn't make sense. We must produce various models in small quantities. An operator who is able to do only a single process can't work well. The operator should be able to operate any process as a professional. The machine is a mere automation system but has to use a man's brain. The line should be available for the production of any model. This flow is from multi-process handling to autonomation to set-up revolution.

### 8.9.1 Multi-Process Handling

One worker should be able to handle multiple processes so that we can manufacture products with lesser number of workers. The worker is trained and educated in one process after another systematically. When we have workers who can handle only one process, you have to prepare a different set for each process and different production volumes. As the worker studies a lot of processes, the desire of skill improvement in his mind springs and becomes involved in the business. This is the most significant point. This is also an education that creates professionals. Let us consider multi-process handling. There are several know-hows to multi-process handling. We reduce human labor as much as possible by operating machines with minimum human intervention. There are interesting steps like hands free, eyes free and human free. The second is one-piece flow and standing work. Sitting work is very difficult for multi-process handling. We eliminate isolated workshops. We reduce machine size and parallel bar-shaped lines to minimize operator movements. We need good work standards and a training plan for multi-skilled operators.

### 8.9.2 Autonomation

The term 'autonomation' comes from the Toyota Production System. It is different from automation. Autonomation doesn't necessarily need higher technology like in the case of automation.

The machine may have its troubles and produce defective products. Even though automation was made for avoiding the operator's work, the operator might have to watch the machine all the time. If automated machines went on operating even when the subsequent processes had stopped due to some reason, it would lead to much inventory in process or chaos.

Autonomation is a system to stop a machine automatically when it is in trouble, or the machine or process in the next stage develops a trouble. Autonomation is a system led by the human brain.

Toyota originally started as a textile machine maker founded by Sakichi Toyoda. The loom was used to make fabric by weaving yarn or thread. The manual operation seldom broke the thread but it took time to tie the longer thread. It is usual that manual weaving takes a longer time because an operator does his job carefully.

An automatic machine for this process was thus developed, which gave higher speed. However, at times, the thread would break, creating defective fabric pieces. This is why an operator had to supervise each machine to stop it whenever a thread broke. In such cases, he had to stop the machine and tie the thread and then restart the machine. He had to always be beside the machine because he had no clue when a thread might break. To overcome the problem, a new machine was invented, which would automatically stop the loom whenever the thread was in trouble. Thus, one operator could be in a position to take care of several machines.

If every machine could stop automatically when the trouble occurred in the machines, parts, products and the next processes, you would not have unnecessary defects or need extra inventory. This is the basis of autonomation. It is a mechanical system with a human brain. Before that, everybody has to understand perfectly that we must not produce dubious quality stuff at any time or when the next process is in trouble.

**Autonomation**

### 8.9.3 Set-Up Revolution

The set-up revolution is an important feature of flexible manpower. We can produce anything, anytime by shortening the set-up time. When the set-up time takes longer, we will need to produce more and consequently keep large inventories. Minimum set-up time makes it possible for us to produce anything, anytime with lesser inventories. When a worker is assigned to the process, the costs remain constant. Large inventories cost more and occupy more space. Large inventories cause tensions in the site preventing quick action against problems in quality, equipment and so on. Lean manufacturing cannot be achieved under large inventories. We will find a very nice example of the set-up in an unexpected place. Have you seen a Formula One race? The machine goes into the pits to change tires and refill fuel. How long does it take to do everything? We don't know the details but they change four tires and refill fuel within a minute. How long does it take for you to change a tire when you have a flat tire? We can find an ideal set-up in F1. Just follow it.

**Motor Sport-Team Play**

1. Team play and clear responsibility of the role

    Each member of the team has his own role and a strong responsibility. The most important role of the members is to cover for someone when they have a trouble. If someone makes a mistake, the whole team would be beaten. This is the professional way of working or thinking.

    Let's consider such occasions. A seller may insist that it was not his fault even though his customer is in trouble. What is going on in such a seller's mind? Not the consideration that his customer is in trouble, but whether it was his fault or not. Everybody in the company has to be a salesman in front of the customer. The person who tells a customer, "It is not my fault," is always thinking of himself instead of his customers. If we have a lot of such employees in the company, we should realize that the condition of the company is very dangerous. We should recognize that we have to educate and train them to behave, saying "I am sorry. I can't answer right now. Please let me call another person who can do it for you."

2. Each member is trained as a professional

Ideally, in a professional environment, all members are always under training and practicing like a fire brigade so that they can respond to any situation.

We should admit that compared to foreign products, some Indian products face more quality problems. The reason why we have so many quality problems is that the fault is in our mind. Each employee may feel little sense of responsibility as a professional. The trouble could be due to designing or manufacturing problems. He doesn't feel any sense of guilt even though a quality problem happens. He may be always busy searching for excuses to establish that it was not his fault.

A real professional takes pride in his products. If he causes a defect in any product in the market, he would feel very ashamed of it. Therefore, he makes his products after careful consideration of various possibilities or scenarios. All members of our company should be professionals and be aware of their professional responsibilities or ethics. We should know that it is the responsibility of top management to transform employees to professionals. Every employee must be totally committed to the needs of the customer.

**A Professional Takes Pride**

3. No wasteful movement from work standards

    The standard work is created after plenty of simulation to eliminate wasteful movements. In Indian manufacturing companies, workers can be seen moving around during a process. The most surprising thing is that a worker can leave the line without any permission from the supervisor. It is very difficult to know where he goes: to the washroom, to drink water or to do something else. Usually, he doesn't come back quickly. This situation shows lack of strict rules and that standard work procedures are not determined or well-controlled.

    Can you imagine what would happen if a worker goes to the washroom when a car is in a pit at F1? All operators of the F1 racing team share a clear and common goal. What percentage of Indian employees identify with the targets of the company? This is also the responsibility of the top management.

4. Offline set-up

    In order to minimize the inline set-up, offline set-up should be done as much as possible. It is nonsensical to take time and travel long distances to find tools. We can produce large varieties with small quantities after the set-up revolution. But we have to understand the need for thorough training. This is also the key part in a company improvement. In order to minimize the on-line time, we need as much offline preparation as possible.

5. Extremely fast on-line set-up

    Industries understand well that the processing is waste and they are minimizing the process. In factories too, there are several methods like zero bolt, one-touch attachment, one-touch alignment and so on. We should aim at 'single minute change-over'.

## 8.10 Other Important Points

### 8.10.1 The Medicine Seller of Toyama

The suburban city named Toyama was famous for a long time for the production and sales of medicine in Japan. The salesmen of pharmaceutical companies in Toyama carried a lot of medicines with them and went to sell at the metropolis in the past. They never opened a shop anywhere in the city. Each salesman visits his customers within his range directly. This is just like probiotic drink maker Yakult sells directly to its users. They send their sales ladies to offices to provide healthy probiotic drink to the customers at their door steps. What he does first is to share a happy story with the customer. And, after some time, he looks into the customer's medicine case and puts only the necessary medicines. He tidies the medicine case so that anybody can see what and how many there are in it, at a glance. His customers would never be without medicines or have any unnecessary medicines. In Japan, a lot of manufacturing companies are making a drastic effort to gather correct information quickly from their customers and the marketing is always in contact with the factory so that they can maintain a stable production rate every day.

In India, there are many such companies and Haldiram is just one example of success.

Haldiram is able to manage and keep their production to provide for each of their sales outlets variety of items and still keep food wastages to minimum.

**Image of Lady Selling Yakult in Japan**

## 8.10.2 Poka-Yoke

*Poka-yoke* used to be called as *baka-yoke*. It meant even a *baka* can't make a mistake. *Baka* means 'fool' in the Japanese language. The term was changed because it was considered vulgar. *Poka* means absent-minded and even those who are not fools can become absent-minded and forgetful at times. The *poka* proof technique is used in several fields. This method is applied in simple devices to advanced technologies.

The first step in *poka-yoke* is 5S. The next is color coding and indicating and so on. These are not necessarily impeccable. At a higher level, a design to avoid wrong part assemblage is introduced. There are many methods for mechanical protection like using pin guides to computer control. Very high-level of engineering is used in case of the *poka-yoke* of aircraft. It must be perfect.

One mistake in an aircraft spells the end. However, despite using sophisticated cutting-edge technology, an aircraft may crash. On the contrary, there are several simple aircraft that have been flying for a long time without accidents. It will be meaningful to create *poka-yoke* ideas. But it would be meaningless if workers become inattentive and end up making another mistake. We should strongly recognize the importance of inculcating intrinsic human values in workers.

On 29th December 1972, the Eastern Airline Flight 401, which took off from New York, JFK, crashed into a swamp before its destination, Miami International Airport in Florida. The aircraft was the newest Lockheed L-1011 Tri-Star, which could land at the airport at full automatic pilot mode. That night, as the plane was approaching Miami International Airport, on full automatic mode, just before landing, the lights in the 'gear down' did not glow. All three pilots in the cockpit had paid attention only to the lamp, and the elbow of a pilot had unconsciously touched the control stick, changing the autopilot mode. The aircraft went out of control, crashed and many became victims.

This is an example that shows even *poka-yoke* can make fools. The three pilots were concentrating only on a dead lamp costing less than ten dollars. We must not allow workers to relax during the process. The device for quality assurance may often prevent operators from applying their mind. In India, there are a lot of workers who may not have the aptitude for quality assurance. We have to create an aptitude in them. There have been many more such happenings since then.

**Flight 401 Crash**

### 8.10.3 Water Spider

As we mentioned under the topic 'Efficiency', one of the reasons for a line stop is material shortage. There can be two situations. One, there is no material at all in the factory. The other, there is no material on the line but it is available at a short distance. In our case, a worker usually leaves the line for getting the parts. He can't work at the line while he is away to pick materials, and naturally, the productivity comes down. Is this the only problem?

In fact, every time there is a shortage of parts, he leaves the line to pick the parts. Thus, he starts thinking he can leave the line anytime. He then leaves his line even for reasons other than shortage of parts including for private matters. He may leave for drinking water but not come back soon. When a machine breaks down, he may go somewhere while the maintenance personnel is attending to it and he does not come back even when the machine is ready. So this line can't be an efficient one.

Machines can't be allowed to break down, and materials should not cause any shortage problem. Despite the breakdown of machines and material shortage, your workers will need to be at the line always. Workers should not be allowed to leave the line, and they must seek the permission of the supervisor before leaving the workplace for any reason, including answering nature's calls. It is the rule. They can leave the line at break and lunchtime only, and they have to return to the line in time after such breaks.

Machine breakdowns should be strictly avoided through proper preventive maintenance and material shortage problem must be stopped by deploying water spider system. The water spider is a specialized material handler, and he should concentrate on providing material to the line only. The water spider species always move quickly. This would help the line workers to fully concentrate on the line without excuse.

In excellent companies in Japan and the Western countries, material shortage seldom happens. They operate well, under the water spider system. But we can see many cases of material shortage in Indian manufacturing factories even though they have material handlers. An Indian material handler is not a water spider who moves always and quickly too. The reason may be the mindset of a material handler in India. First of all, he doesn't understand the importance of 'first in and first out' and he doesn't feel any sense of responsibility regarding material shortage. There is no rule on how many times and how often he should supply the parts, and he would supply as many as possible at a time so that he can take time out for relaxing and idling away, sometimes even forgetting to come back, leading to more problems.

As he doesn't understand the critical points, he can't recognize or predict the timing of material shortage. His mind is set not on doing good work but on finding idling time. Top management of India's manufacturing companies must understand the purpose and the rules of water spider system and its true meaning. Otherwise, we may have always two contradictory problems—over inventory and material shortage. Workers must keep on working except during breaks.

**A Water Spider**

*"The key to the Toyota Way and what makes Toyota stand out is not any individual elements–but what is important is having all elements together as system. It must be practiced every day in a very consistent manner, not in spurts"*

Taiichi Ohno
Founder Toyota Production System

*"The Toyota style is not to create results by working hard. It is a system that says there is no limit to people's creativity. People don't go to Toyota to 'work' they go there to 'think'"*

Taiichi Ohno
Founder Toyota Production System

# –9–

# How Do We Succeed in India?

## 9.1 How Much Ability Does a Human Being Have?

There are plenty of people in the world. They say an Indian baby who was born on 31$^{st}$ October 2011 was the seven billionth person. We are now 7.7 billion and still growing beyond 1%. Among them, some can show their abilities most satisfactorily, while others can't. We can say that Olympic athletes, big businessmen, and other great persons are those who can show their abilities.

But how about ordinary people? They can't utilize more than 90 percent of their abilities. God has given all of us excellent abilities. Have you ever thought how much ability each of us has? In case of an identical twin, one of them can sense what is happening to the other—who may be at far away.

In Japan, they call it "incredible strength during a fire". A human being can exhibit enormous strength carrying heavy furniture or holding on to their family, which he can't normally do during an emergency. Let me share an incident.

In a country, a middle-aged lady once found a baby who was about to fall from a balcony of an apartment building. "Oh! My God," she said and tried hard to rush to the point and succeeded in catching him. Thus, she could save the baby. The baby was not injured at all. This lady was wearing a pair of sandals. Later on, a thorough inspection of the scene was carried out. The distance she had run and the height from which the baby had dropped were measured. Calculations were made repeatedly and it was finally confirmed that the lady had been faster than the male world record holder for the 100-meter sprint, at that time.

God has given an excellent ability to each of us. But we can't utilize the abilities due to our negligence and inadequate efforts. Evil thoughts like greed, envy and jealousy disturb us from recognizing our potential. The lady with the sandals did not bother about her non-athletic body but she fully concentrated on helping the baby.

Concentration of mind enables us to exhibit our potential. Distraction won't help us. We have a million times power than we may think. Only we have not been able to show it yet and we may need to put in more effort to do so. We must think of harnessing the human power than about cheap labor. We should fully utilize our talents, abilities, knowledge and zeal to ensure the growth of our organization and society. Lower manpower cost should be only an additional advantage.

## 9.2 Why Can't Human Beings Communicate Well?

We like to take some examples of how animals differ from human beings for trouble free communication. We can analyze from various points of views. Lets take example of emotion say love! Animals don't show emotions like human beings do. While Human beings have complex emotions and can continue to cherish emotions for posterity. All of us cherish and enjoy family's love or comfort. On the other hand the activity of an animal is determined by their instincts. In absence of any language capability like human being, they may have other ways of expressing their feelings.

Does it means animals adhere to rules better than human beings? Animals are always sticking to work standards. But God has created such emotions inside human being, which is a rather intricate trick. God may thus appear miraculous. Just consider.

You dropped a coin on the ground. The coin rolled like a monocycle and then escaped into the narrow clearance between the furniture and the wall.

It seemed like your hand could almost reach it, but ultimately it couldn't. A bar found nearby was almost reachable, but it wasn't. On a very important day, you needed to wake up early. But the battery of alarm clock failed and it did not ring.

All these are part miracles of God.

On the other hand there are no traffic accidents in the world of animals. Have you ever seen the formation flight of gray starlings? Every animal acts according to the rules determined by instinct, and it can keep up with any complicated movement. But, unfortunately, God has also made devils that live within human beings in the form of various emotions like greed, jealousy, laziness and self-satisfaction.

As many human beings are conquered by these internal devils, they never agree on a meaningful goal. They are defeated by the temptations of easy benefits and lethargy. Human beings have been given excellent abilities by God, but he voluntarily gives up the license to use them.

It's the reason why human beings can't communicate well owing to such mental turbulences, while animals can do it perfectly. If we want to improve ourselves, we have to defeat the devils living in us. And you must make the most use of another gift from God, which is hope. In the company, we need more *HouRenSou* to report, inform and consult freely.

**Formation Flight of Birds Never Collide**

## 9.3 Equality Among Humans and in Profession

There are many people who are lazy in Japan and Western countries as well. They can never succeed in business. Succeeding in business is comparable to succeeding in sports, and we can't win without sufficient practice. There is a concept of caste in India but there was *Shi-Nou-Kou-Shou* class discrimination a long time ago in Japan too. Now there's no such discrimination. Caste is a system based on traditional occupations. The traditional professions are not problematic. The problem with India, just like what existed in Japan in the past, is the segregation of human beings into two segments: to be respected and to be despised. The sun is shining on human beings equally on the planet; do we have to look down upon people whom we have never met? Each human being has his own ability, which is given by God and he has to do his duty. We have to express our appreciation toward people who work for us. It would be a very simple matter to understand if we imagine we are living alone in an uninhabited island. A Japanese consultant says there are no inferior jobs in the world. Every work requires a technique. As the technique improves, the competitiveness of our country's products will increase too. Keeping the society and workplace clean and tidy is a good technique. The countries with competitive products are keeping their societies clean and neat. Unless we keep the workplace and public places clean and neat, we don't have sufficient global competence.

Globally, excellent companies like Toyota begin education of their employees by telling them about their role as a diligent member of the society. In Japan and Germany, not only workplaces but public places are also kept clean and neat always. They have engineered techniques on how not to dirty the places or how to clean efficiently because they know that this is the fundamental power behind all development.

Sometimes we see the behavior of some Indians who seem to be thinking, "I can dirty my society because there are other guys to scavenge." What happiness do housekeepers derive from cleaning the place dirtied by a guy? They know very well that they are not respected. We in India should identify the necessity of awareness revolution in the entire society for the development of the industry. Simply imitating successful methods, seeking cheap labor and laidback ways will not improve technology or increase competence. Now what we need is hard work. The *swacchata* movement started recently is a great initiative, and involves massive work. It can succeed only if the entire population of the country participates in it and ensures proper implementation. This will create an environment and foundation to build world-class organizations, which can follow business excellence practices.

## 9.4 Bottom-Up Industries

As we mentioned before, there is a system named VLFM, supported by the Japanese government, for India's industrial development. In this system sponsored by JICA, many of India's top management learn Japanese management systems. We believe this system has brought great results.

When Japanese Prime Minister Shinzo Abe visited India in 2007, he was asked by former president Kalam to help bottom-up India's manufacturing industries. As the bottom-up development is not easily achievable through foreign support, the conclusion was to begin with top management change, and the system was started. Apart from the companies that can attend this program, there are plenty of small size companies in India. We think India's economic development in real meaning is extremely difficult unless we raise these companies as well. This is the responsibility of politicians and the top management of leading companies.

The scenario in India's economic development is like this. A lot of Indian critics may oppose it. What Indian people have to do is to learn what personal quality and quality of enterprises are. We don't necessarily need to introduce foreign capital, but we must learn how they have succeeded. This way, introduction of foreign capital may be very effective. It may be effective in special circumstances such as when we introduce capital of a foreign company, which will bring back the products made in India. This is because, in such a case, the products will be evaluated according to global standards. Exports will provide domestic benefits. Unless we learn about what the quality of our products and services should be, India's economic growth will be limited. We understand that India's IT industry paid attention to countries from across the world and has been very much contributing to India's economic development. The Indian government should focus more on agriculture and small companies in the manufacturing sector. The Indian government is already doing this under the 'Make in India' campaign.

We think it is the duty of Government of India to educate the majority of population who are in-charge of agriculture and small businesses. They should become the people who can produce and provide the finest products as a mission. This is the real *monozukuri*. A real manager can stimulate power from the bottom.

## 9.5 Power of Dreams

The basis of quality and service is the attitude to avoid putting others in trouble and making others (customers) happy. The most important thing is that we have to always think of ways to study at home, school and organizations. Business runners should have their goals set and share them with all the employees.

It is better in the sports world. The goals are clear to understand like a gold medal in Olympic Games or a victory at the World Cup. All members are pursuing the same goal, and it is easy to rally powers. The battle is only against laziness, and an efficient hard worker can easily win. We are driven by the power of a strong longing. This is the power of dream. What about your organization or company?

The budget of the government should be the top policy of the country, but many nationals do not empathize and throw cold water on the plan. Even in a private company, a similar situation could exist. Even though the top management sets a goal like doubling the sales, it is very rare to see all employees striving toward the goal. The enterprise that can utilize the power of dream is very strong. Globally excellent companies are very good at utilizing the power of dream. You may say it's easy but it is very difficult in India because being a democratic country people hold different viewpoints. There are very few examples in India where companies have worked together to become global leaders in their sectors. However, the culture of continuous improvement has still not made an impact in smaller and medium-size organizations.

A society that allows free competition is also one that allows dreams to come true. What do we want to become? What do we want to do? We have a concrete dream. We need not mind if our family is laughing at us, or our friends are mocking at us. The important thing is that we have a clear and concrete dream. The famous Japanese space astronaut Mr. Mamoru Mori has been insisting on kids to dreams on their own. Is living without a dream happier than sleeping on the road? Excepting some northern provinces in India, living on the road is not fatal.

But there are some Indians who are pursuing their dreams. Athletes who aim to win at the Olympic Games are very distinct. They set targets to realize the dream. "I want to become a gold medalist at the age of **. In order to do that, I will set **% of the world record as the target. I will make a long-term plan from now on. I will make a monthly plan, breaking down the long-term plan."

How about the coaching staff? According to the detailed plan on the method of practice, training place, cash flow and so on, he trains and watches the games. His target is always the same: To win a gold medal in his **th year. If he falls behind the schedule, he tries to find out the reason, and if he remains ahead of the schedule, he rechecks whether the plan is too easy. Through hard work, the athlete who puts in the effort is almost sure to win. Athletes who win a silver or bronze medal feel the sense of achievement. These are really strong persons. They are not those who are sleeping on the road. The products and services such persons provide can satisfy global customers, as they can engage the audience in the stadium.

We have to be thoroughly aware and charged up, enabling employees to reap the advantages by making your dream come true. Outsourced housekeepers are not exceptions. It is not the privilege of a limited number of managers to enjoy the happiness by achieving the dream. These organizations will surely collapse. The difference between people with dreams and without them is quite large. A man with a dream makes an effort to achieve his dream. He reflects on the cause behind an unexpected result. He will be able to arrive at a new method after his reflection. This is the energy that makes human grow. This is called diligence. Diligent people frequently face hardships.

A man without dreams doesn't need to make an effort to achieve his dream. He wants to escape from hardship. As he has little experience of hardship, he can't grow as a human being. There are a lot of such people in the world. Only a few people have dreams in the world. And only a section of these people will make the effort to fulfil their dreams.

A person may speak volumes about his dreams, but it doesn't come true due to his laziness. He doesn't realize this and blames it on misfortune or another easy excuse. In the worst case, he blames his parents or teachers for their failure in educating him properly. The responsibility of top management is to set a dream and share it with all related workers.

## 9.6 Power of Love

All of us have the power of love to draw out the deep powers from within us. This power of love makes us do anything for anyone we hold dear. Once in love, an individual starts thinking of what he wants to do for his dear ones. The imagination expands and fills with possibilities of actions that help people they care for. They may imagine situations where a trouble may befall a loved one. "You will get late! You can't do that thing right now!" "Be careful, or else you may be injured!"

The strong passion we feel for our loved ones makes us imagine impending dangers and take action extremely calmly and boldly for fear of losing them. When all the members in an organization love each other, the problems within can be identified quickly and solved. People in India are very family-oriented and the same passion we have for family should be cultivated among organization members.

The capitalist world is the world of competition. Competition leads to wisdom and helps in improving technologies. India's socialist market before 1991 wasn't conducive for technological advancement. If we want to lower the cost, we can make the vendors compete. We should employ the cheapest vendor. This is often done in Europe and America as well.

The Nano project of Tata also seems to have followed this system. There is the school of thought in Japan called *keiretsu*. The vendor is decided at the first project by the competitiveness in quality, cost and credibility of his company, but once adopted, the vendor will continue to be a partner for a long time. This is like the idea of lifetime employment. When a vendor enters one of the enterprise groups, he will be treated as a member of the family. A member of the family becomes an object of familial love. From this time onwards, the severity or brutality of competition will change to the whip of love in quality and cost.

It'll be surprising to visit the Toyota Company in Japan and find a vendor being treated as a guest. Generally, in any country, the material department that contacts vendors is shabby and most vendors are repulsed by the staff of the material department. They (i.e. the staff of material division) often look down upon the vendors' personnel. In the case of Toyota Company, vendors, as well as customers, are treated as family. In such a case, vendors can sense the love, discover problems immediately and solve them quickly with the help of others in the family.

When they encounter a disaster, despite not having extra inventories, they can fix it in no time at all with the help of the family. They are expected to make daily efforts to produce more power of love. We need to utilize the power of love as much as possible.

## 9.7 Power of Direction

A Japanese consultant's house in Japan suffered damage from the East Japan Great Earthquake Disaster in March 2011. The Fukushima Daiichi Nuclear Power Plant of Tokyo Electric Power suffered a big damage from tsunami. They were still struggling with leaking polluted water, as the plant was destroyed. There was no power supply for two days to his house, from the day of the earthquake. After the power supply resumed, no power stop has ever happened since.

When the disaster broke out, the Japanese consultant was fortunately in India. But his wife was seized with a terror that she had never experienced before. She had to endure more than two days in the house where all furniture was overturned and broken glass lay scattered, without power and water. When a water supply truck came, a line of more than 300 meters was formed. But no one tried to sneak ahead of the line or complained. During such disasters, some confusion may generally happen. Sometimes a riot may break out. But people can join forces together, aligning themselves in the same direction, and they can get a big power to achieve seemingly impossible things. We can be proud of the incident where many Indians joined together to help a baby elephant that had fallen into a pond.

Say one person has only a power of 50 kg. If five persons use these powers in the same direction, then the total power can become 250 kg. But, in most cases, each person uses his power promiscuously as he likes. As a result, no power is conserved, resulting in the exhaustion of everybody. Unless we can gain the desired result, we think there is no point in sporadic efforts. We can produce the effect when we work together toward an organization. The organization makes rules in order to achieve its purpose.

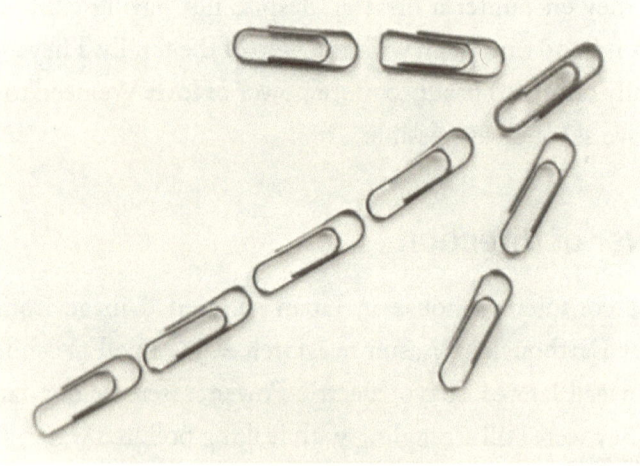

**Direction of Efforts**

It is the duty of every employee to adhere to rules. A big power can be generated if all members of the organization perform their duties. Once we find ourselves producing a result that is different from the target, we can amend the rules. You can start afresh according to the new rules. But human beings are imperfect. The devil lives with us inside our body. This devil is may be in different forms like envy, jealousy, dissatisfaction, laziness and so on. There are a lot of people who are defeated by such devils. They think, "I don't follow the rule because I don't like it. I don't follow the rule because it puts others at a advantage. I don't follow rules because it is bothersome." We need to work hard to create the direction. The top management has to show the clear target and work hard for the leadership.

> *"All of us do not have equal talent. Yet, all of us have an equal opportunity to develop our talents"*
>
> **Ratan Tata**

> *"I am defined by my curiosity and thirst for learning. I buy more books than I can finish. I sign up for more online courses than I can complete. I fundamentally believe that if you are not learning new things, you stop doing great and useful things"*
>
> **Satya Nadella**

# –10–

# AN ORGANIZATION THAT MAY BE SUCCESSFUL IN THE GLOBAL MARKET

Why don't we try to make an image of a successful organization in the world? This is not a surreal thing. Shouldn't we aim at creating such an organization?

## 10.1 Safety First

Safety is the first priority of every employee. Safety includes good health. All employees must realise that should an accident occur, it would not only affect the person concerned, but also his family, his colleagues, the organization and the nation. The organization should conduct regular training and safety education. All employees are obliged to submit 'safety potential' suggestions, highlighting hidden risks to sustain the degree of their interest in safety. The organization keeps a record of these, compiles the data and takes actions through visual control. Everyone must participate in safety audits regularly. The entire organisation should daily learn about safety failures elsewhere and take suitable steps to avoid recurrence.

The organization creates a safety standard. All employees follow the standard. Any employee who doesn't comply with this criterion shall be cautioned and trained to strictly follow safety rules. Employees not adhering to rules may not be encouraged to remain in company. When a newcomer joins this organization, this matter must clearly be explained to him and a counter signature must be taken as a token of consent or acceptance. Whenever an accident happens inside or outside the organization, the event, cause and action shall be discussed in the safety meeting. The cause shall then be traced to the root cause.

Every employee is first a citizen of the country and a key member of the society. All employees should be educated on various safety violations happening outside the premises of the company.

**Safety First**

## 10.2 Thoroughness of 5S

To highlight again it is repeated that no one can dirty the premises of their organization. Employees must not defile the facilities of the organization—floors, machineries, warehouses, offices and toilets included. What is recognized as trash should be put inside the trash box. The trash boxes and toilets must be always kept clean. Members of the committee must patrol the premises every day and deal with violations or exceptions severely.

Desks and cabinets you use must be kept nicely organized as part of your responsibility and should be always clean and neat. Common equipment and cabinets must be cleaned and tidied up by users in turns. At the workplace, equipment must be cleaned by the operator. When a work shift finishes, the operator must clean his machine not only on the surface but also inside, including the control panel. Have a fixed timing for every member to clean his office or workshop. A member who is working and not cleaning during this period shall be penalized.

In India's manufacturing industry, the cleaning techniques are very primitive. According to a Japanese consultant, nobody considers cleaning a technology. This is because of the notion that cleaning should be done by housekeepers. We may not be able to learn engineering if we keep our workplace filthy. When they are told to clean the workplace dirtied by chips, they blow them off using compressed air. They don't care where the chips go. The flying chip may land on a component or subcomponent and create a quality problem. If we try to clean an electric circuit board using compressed air, we would damage the board with the moisture in the compressed air. This aspect is beyond the housekeeper's territory and he doesn't touch it. On the other hand, the operator doesn't think of cleaning as part of his duty. So nobody cleans the machine or its panel. The operator must clean his machine carefully like adoring your child with affection. We must not use compressed air during such cleaning. When you have to use it, you should be mindful of its disadvantages. The vacuum cleaner is the most effective for cleaning. The suction engineering is used in a lot of processes to keep parts intact all over the world.

But a foreigner often says it is difficult to find a good quality vacuum cleaner in India. This may be an indication that cleaning is being neglected in India. A Japanese consultant points out this culture may be preventing India's manufacturing industry from developing. Demand alone doesn't make a business successful. Quality problems like rejections in a factory or in the field are caused by dirt, chip and such abnormalities. As many advanced industries in the world have experienced, just cleaning a dirty factory can improve the quality level drastically. In the factory that only displays names, posters or banners of 5S, they are always struggling with quality problems like poor conductivity due to dirt, mixing up wrong parts, short circuit and so on. The culture that deems it the housekeeper's job to clean seems to hinder the improvement of engineering production quality.

In Japan, there is a group of housekeepers who are called 'Angels'. They clean bullet trains. Two old lady housekeepers are assigned for a coach and they wait for an oncoming bullet train. They greet passengers alighting from the train, and, with a garbage bag, they clean and shift seat sides under 7 minutes. One coach has more than 100 seats. They not only do housekeeping but marketing work as well. India is now going to introduce Japanese *Shinkansen*. Is India also going to introduce these 'Angels' in the Indian *Shinkansen*?

**5S Activity, Angels at Work**

## 10.3 The Organization to Speak on Dreams

The top members of the organization must communicate its dream every 6 months to all employees. They must reflect on the results of the previous 6 months. They must talk about the dream of expansion in sales and profits, methods to achieve it, the challenges, importance of solidarity among employees, the harmfulness of defaulting, preciousness of compliance, meaninglessness of individual crime and respectful contribution to the society. They must create happiness through which all employees can achieve the common dream.

China is now leading against India in economy. However, there is a great possibility that India can catch up with China in a few years. India is the largest democratic country and it stands for its magnanimity. We know many of India's excellent companies already let their employees dream as clearly as possible. However, we think, India's small and middle-class manufacturers should recognize it as the most welcome change to happen.

Every member of an organization can have a common dream and discuss it with each other any time.

**Speak about Dreams**

## 10.4 The Organization That Makes the Most of Education

An organization always plans and takes efforts toward education of its employees. Education has two aspects: mental and technical. The mental education should be given the first preference. For example: educating how to behave as a human being. We have a lot of things to comprehend before learning how not to put others in trouble. The importance of making an effort and the harmfulness of an easy-going attitude may be included in the curriculum. Challenging the stronger ones and caring for the weaker ones should also be part of the education. We should educate them about waste too. Many good organizations in India are also educating employees about insurance, personal health, social work and CSR, which other industries must also follow.

Regarding technical education, we must pick the subjects carefully, and training should be repeated and results confirmed through examination. Though some employees may leave the organization after education or training, these efforts need not be directed toward retaining them in the organization. We should understand that the organization is not attractive enough to retain employees. We should make more effort toward making the organization more attractive.

Regardless of what one may believe, those who trouble others are disliked. Speaking loudly in public, listening to music without earphones, sneaking ahead in a line, not paying money, breaking a promise – a person with such habits can't get along with others, globally. He won't be trusted or get business. He may get lucky for a while, but it won't last.

Regardless of their beliefs, the ones who don't make an effort won't be rewarded. A carefree attitude will never achieve anything. We can sleep on the road, but we are not allowed to sleep in the organization. No God promotes a lazy man. Only those who make an effort will see results and be rewarded in the organization.

Regardless of one's beliefs, a human being must have a challenging spirit to become stronger. The challenging spirit makes a person do physical exercises and helps him keep fit thereby, making his spirit stronger. If we have a heart that cares for the weak, we may start thinking with a broader wider perspective, and more generously. If we always think selfishly and narrow-mindedly, we can't arrive at the best solution. We will see things clearly and broadly from a distance, taking a step back, without being near-sighted.

Regardless of one's beliefs, they should study waste. Profit making companies and the government may have different definitions for the term; there is not a big difference. Waste doesn't exist without a purpose. If we have a clear purpose, we can start discussing wastes. If managers and employees have a common purpose, it is not so difficult to minimize wastage in an organization. An employee's purpose is occasionally different from a manager's. The purpose may mean values. While the manager thinks about productivity enhancement, the employee thinks about higher wages for easier work. An indiscreet manager misunderstands that he belongs to the privileged class, where one rarely finds wastes. Managers should discover and divert waste toward the purpose. Employees understand that their most important contribution is to observe the rules that managers decided on. This is the manager's most important obligation. Managers have to convince employees to achieve the highest happiness by working as professionals. Why don't we recognize again that the enterprise consists of persons?

**Education**

## 10.5 Accurate Information Management

All employees must know the meaning of the information. Information within the organization must be managed correctly. We must reply within a minute when an outsider seeks a small piece of information. We must detect wastes through accurate information and minimize them. A foreigner can't help but doubt the reliability of information he receives, although India is an IT power. We do not keep our appointments. We say 5 minutes, but it may take more than 30 minutes. A car that signals right turn may make a left turn. Most drivers don't use indicators. According to our analysis, many of India's drivers may make little use of indicators and their technique of using one is poor compared to other advanced countries.

They go through traffic without signaling and steering appropriately and forcefully intimidate other vehicles and pedestrians using horns. Horns and indicators are not for us but for the benefit of other vehicles and pedestrians. It is awfully wrong to use them in a wrong way and as a weapon. The society or the organization doesn't work because of us alone. In order to make a society or organization work, exchange of information is awfully important. We can't make a proper judgment unless we get correct information instantly. In this respect, animals are far more excellent than human beings. A herd of elephants moves exchanging information properly and the formation of a flight of birds is excellent. As they are exchanging information accurately and instantly, no accident happens. India ranks first in the number of deaths caused by traffic accidents around the world. The causes are many, but we think we should try and improve our attitude toward the accuracy of information we give.

**Accurate Information**

## 10.6 A Group of Professionals

All employees, including outsourced housekeepers, must be professionals because they are being paid. Everybody must take pride in their jobs and they may demand compensation according to their accomplishment. They should not demand compensation on account of anything else. Professional sports players like cricketers always compete aggressively and study and practice daily to improve their skill and technique. This hard work leads to an increase in their income. Whatever the job is, professionals should compete with each other by improving their abilities every day. Whatever the process is, we must set a target to improve efficiency. We are not allowed to deliver any rejects to the next process. Professionals should not hand over any rejects to others. Indirect, direct and outsourced employees must be professional and be treated equally.

If we raise compensation without any achievement, we may promote lazy employees. The targets to be achieved should be communicated and understood clearly; otherwise, we may have a tough wage negotiation.

## 10.7 Be Mindful of Gratitude

The organization must not forget to express its gratitude toward employees for the profit made due to their effort. We must consider suitable distribution of the profit toward internal reserve, investment, rewards to employees, social contribution and so on. Top management who think they are making profit only as the result of the executives' effort will surely fail in future. We must use a part of the money earned through profit for improvement of society, especially the areas that are not covered adequately by the government. We think education is one such problematic area in India. When we gain profit, there are many possibilities of investing in awareness revolution on town cleaning, prevent honking, campaigns to remodel toilets in schools, and providing aid for children who can't go to school. The government is making an effort to educate everyone, collecting money in the form of education tax. But money and human resources are absolutely in short supply. If the number of children who come to school increases, or the quality of education improves, future market expansion and India's economic development can be achieved and profits realized. You would repent in future if you thought only about the present. We should also educate our employees to be grateful to the organization.

**Express Gratitude**

## 10.8 Be Proud of You

Each employee must be proud of himself. He should internally feel:

- My organization is the most beautiful one.
- My organization can provide the best services in the world.
- My organization can provide the best quality products in the world.
- My organization can be cost-effective and the strongest in the world.

Each employee must take the above seriously. Why don't we replace organization with India?

We may build such an organization gradually and win the admiration of Indian and foreign businessmen. In the first stage, it may very difficult due to the difficulties involved in an awareness revolution, but a small effort or beginning may help us move up slowly. Adopting a culture that does not imitate others and creating original products and services may soon help absorb the twelve million pass-outs each year.

**Be Proud of Yourself**

*"Take up one idea. Make that one idea your life – think of it, dream of it, and live on that idea. Let the brain, muscles, nerves, every part of your body, be full of that idea, and just leave every other idea alone. This is the way to success"*

Swami Vivekananda

# –11–

# CLOSING

It is not easy to have one common strategy for a multi-ethnic, multilingual, multi-religious and diverse nation as India. But the road to the great future is right in front of us. Diversity can become the biggest strength of youngsters in India, enabling them to become world leaders. Toyota went to Ford to study cost reduction and, at the same time, it learned about imaging future goals. India is expected to have a great future thanks to its abundant resources and young population.

Japan passed through great hardship after World War II, and yet, due to persistent efforts and strategy, it has emerged as one of the world' largest economy. Japan doesn't have the poor class that India has. Japanese call their lowest income class 'poor'. Even the lowest income there is much higher than the average income in India. It means the wages of Japanese people have climbed up. As the cost competitiveness of Japan decreased and much of the manufacturing shifted to China and other Asian countries, where the wages are low, Japan is suffering from the hollowing out of industries. The yen value has increased to 113 yen Vs $ as against 360 yen Vs $ in 1970. Japan has made good quality products and exported them to create more riches and, consequently, the yen value appreciated. The high value of yen has become a headache for the current Japanese economy.

India is blessed with in all aspects. India is still growing at around 7 percent and it is a country of opportunities. Its demographic advantages and fast urbanisation can result in an economic boom. We are self-sufficient in food and we have abundant natural resources. We can export anything: food, manufacturing goods and services. But it only works if we can provide high-quality products and services. Higher valuation of rupee due to export expansion will give us more ability to improve the efficiency. In order to do this, awareness revolution, to create professionals who can provide customers with good products, is required. **Awareness and education to always think of customers first is the priority.** Through the expansion of export, the income of the middle class increases and stimulates the domestic market, and the economy expands. The prosperity of the IT industry contributed to the rise of the middle class. Further development is expected through an awareness revolution, creating professional who are warm-hearted. If we teach them to take pride in their professions and bring them up to put themselves in the customers' shoes, not only IT, but manufacturing and agriculture segments and their products and services will also improve in quality levels and the economy will develop.

We must not forget that there are many young people who dream and support India to achieve its rightful future. The biggest challenge for this country should be educating and training the young people, creating the right mindset and spreading professional knowledge. If we can raise more young people who care about others, study hard and are willing to make the effort, India can become the world leader sooner or later.

Adopting and implementing improvement programmes using tools alone will not help. Bringing cultural change in the organization by ensuring development of all individuals and then using collective wisdom for the benefits of customers is the key for sustainable growth.

It is now time for you to change and move ahead in the globally competitive environment.

The world is moving fast and transforming, as the fourth Industrial Revolution is setting in. Sweeping changes will change the way we have been working. With robotics and AI dominating the scene, a lot of advantages we had will diminish. Clearly, we have to skill our talent, redeploy our talent and provide higher value to customers for survival. While organizations will develop their own strategies, at the individual level you must change now for becoming better professionals and improve every day.

**If we take our steps right, we can rewrite the rules of industry.**

> *"Never stop fighting until you arrive at your destined place – that is, the unique you. Have an aim in life, continuously acquire knowledge, work hard, and have the perseverance to realize the great life"*
>
> Dr. A.P.J. Abdul Kalam

# NOTE

www.ingramcontent.com/pod-product-compliance
Lightning Source LLC
Chambersburg PA
CBHW030759180526
45163CB00003B/1091